A COMPLETELY NEW LOOK AT
INTERRACIAL SEXUALITY

A COMPLETELY NEW LOOK AT INTERRACIAL SEXUALITY

Public Opinion and Select Commentaries

Lawrence R. Tenzer, Ed. D.

SCHOLARS' PUBLISHING HOUSE

1990

Published by Scholars' Publishing House
CN 3000, Manahawkin, New Jersey 08050

© 1990 by Lawrence R. Tenzer, Ed. D.

Library of Congress Catalog Card Number 90-63946

ISBN 0-9628348-1-5

Printed in the United States of America

And ye shall know the truth,
and the truth shall make you free.

John 8.32

Table of Contents

List of Plates

Preface

I would like to begin by stating that this book grew out of my academic background. My doctoral dissertation was entitled, "The Process of Imagination in John Dewey's Philosophy of Aesthetic Experience" (Univ. of Illinois, 1977). This inquiry into the mental process of imagination synthesized with many years of study in the social sciences, and a particular curiosity was born. This curiosity was based on my own personal observations about race relations in contemporary American society, a society in which social mores dictate our interracial boundaries and separate people by imposing a stigma on interracial sexual relations. In spite of these social mores, such sexuality *is* a part of our American culture as illustrated, for example, by the discussion on *The Oprah Winfrey Show* entitled, "Black Men/White Women" (transcript #749 July 27, 1989), and the television interracial romances on *The Robert Guillaume Show, General Hospital,* and *True Colors.*

In pursuing this curiosity about the parameters our society has placed on interracial sexuality, I have coupled my knowledge of the imagination with my knowledge of the social sciences. Many of the observations I have been able to make were influenced by my professional affiliations, among which I might mention the American Sociological Association, the Society for the Psychological Study of Social Issues, the Institute for Advanced Philosophic Research, the Southern Historical Association, the Association for the Study of Afro-American Life and History, the Sex Education and Information Council of the United States, and the Shakespeare Oxford Society. In spite of my academic training, this book has been written with the lay reader in mind.

I have had my personal curiosity about various interracial sexual issues in America satisfied and wish to share what I have found out. It is my most sincere desire that this information may serve as a vehicle by which the personal curiosities of others will be satisfied as well. The quest for knowledge of all kinds continues to be a great pursuit of human beings, and as imagination is replaced with understanding, society advances. This text, then, is offered as a new beginning, both in the microcosm of individual thinking and in the macrocosm of societal thinking.

On a personal note, I must relate that during my writing, I was often asked, "You write about interracial sexual relations. Are you promoting them?" The answer to this question is, "No." Interracial sexual relations are being discussed, not promoted. Readers who choose to think of discussion as a synonym for promotion have entirely missed the point.

Introduction

The contents of this book present a completely new look at interracial sexuality. This completely new look is a combination of two related parts: the first consists of a nation-wide public opinion telephone survey which addresses the current beliefs of American white women, and the second is made up of commentaries (along with notes) which enlarge the scope of these beliefs by considering them within the contexts of the past as well as the present.

The author designed ten belief statements covering a wide range of issues concerned with interracial sexuality in America. Part One presents the findings of a national probability sample of white women who were asked to respond to each of these statements. Other studies that have been done on interracial sexual issues have focused in on couples directly involved in interracial dating and marriage, however, this study provides an entirely different perspective because it surveyed a population at large that was *not* directly involved in such interracial relationships.

Part Two presents eight sociohistorical commentaries which examine the beliefs about interracial sexuality referred to in Part One. These inquiries contain many original and atypical ideas, some of which tend to challenge traditional interpretations and accepted current thinking. *Webster's New World Dictionary of the American Language* defines "commentaries" as "a series of explanatory notes or remarks." It is to be noted, therefore, that each commentary will give insight and provoke thought but in no way attempt to address all aspects of a subject.

This book is the first of its kind on interracial sexual issues in America. Its unique design combines the public opinion of others along with the commentaries of an author. The combination of these two perspectives should prove both enjoyable and enlightening.

PART ONE:

PUBLIC OPINION

1

BACKGROUND AND METHODOLOGY

The survey presented in this book is truly a landmark in the field of public opinion research because it is the very first to focus in on a national probability sample of American white women and their beliefs concerning interracial sexuality. *This particular group was selected as the subject for study because the issue of white women dating and marrying black men has always been at the center of the controversy surrounding interracial sexual relations in America.* The beliefs of white men, black women, and black men as other populations at large are valid as well, but in order to limit the scope of the present study their beliefs had to be left for future research.

A question commonly asked about this public opinion survey has to do with the number of white women who were interviewed. The number was 444, that is to say, a carefully selected national probability sample of 444. Years ago it was discovered that the mere size of a sample was not nearly as important as how the sample was selected. For example, George Gallup reported on a national sample "containing proper proportions of the various population groups" and found that a sample of 442 yielded substantially the same results as a sample of 12,494. He cited another survey in which a sample of 500 mirrored the responses of 30,000 (*A Guide to Public Opinion Polls,* 2d ed. [Princeton, 1948], pp. 14-16). Even if a small sample is carefully selected, well-balanced, and representative, how can it so closely parallel a much larger sample? The answer is found in the laws of probability first established by the Swiss mathematician Jacques Bernoulli (published posthumously in 1713). The following example will serve to illustrate the idea of probability: first, imagine 75,000 blue marbles and 25,000 red marbles together in a large container, and 750 blue marbles and 250 red marbles in a small container; next, imagine all of the marbles in each of the containers being thoroughly mixed up; finally, imagine yourself with your eyes closed picking 100 marbles out of each of the containers. The probability of you selecting 75 blue marbles and 25 red marbles from each container is virtually the same. The important factor in this illustration is the *quality* of each sample rather than its numerical size.

The nation-wide telephone survey presented herein was based on a high quality sample of 444 white women obtained by Opinion Research Corporation of Princeton, New Jersey. This company was especially commissioned to secure the sample as well as collect and tabulate the survey data. The survey was conducted from July 7th through July 9th, 1989.

A few words regarding the company and its specific role are in order here. Opinion Research Corporation was founded in 1938 by Dr. Claude Robinson, previously the Associate Director of the Gallup Poll. The firm is a nationally known premier research organization with branch offices in Chicago, San Francisco, Washington, D. C., and Cambridge, Mass. It must be understood that the commission of Opinion Research Corporation was strictly limited to the acquisition of the national probability sample, data collection, and data tabulation. Nothing more. The precision and thoroughness with which these assignments were completed proved that the reputation and credentials which preceded this company were well-justified. The author alone was responsible for the original idea of conducting this survey, all phases of the design and construction of the survey statements, all aspects of analysis and interpretation, statistical or otherwise, and all other arrangements and presentations. Due to the sensitive sexual nature of several of the survey statements, Opinion Research Corporation was instructed to use only female telephone interviewers. The use of both female and male interviewers would have resulted in same-sex and opposite-sex interviews and would have been inconsistent.

Any public opinion survey will only be as valid and projectable to the public at large as the sample on which it is based, and Opinion Research Corporation acquired a national probability sample of the highest quality. Their National Telephone Sample produced a self-weighting stratified random sample of telephone households by using a form of survey technique known as Random Digit Dialing. Quoting directly from the Opinion Research Corporation sampling methodology without getting too technical with secondary particulars, the basic procedures utilized were as follows:

... Using 1980 Census Data, all counties in the contiguous

United States were grouped into one of thirty-one strata based on median housing value, racial composition, and degree of urbanization. The counties were arranged within each stratum based on geographical proximity and median housing value. Area code/prefix combinations were arranged within each county by geographical proximity. This resulted in the stratification of all active residential area code/prefix combinations. One thousand area code/prefixes were selected in a stratified random manner from this ordered list. [The company goes on to explain,] When a national probability sample is needed for a survey, four-digit random numbers are appended to each of the 1,000 previously selected area code/prefix combinations. The resulting ten-digit numbers are checked to determine if they fall within a bank of working residential numbers. All numbers that might be residential are retained for use. Each telephone number is printed on a separate call record card....The cards containing the telephone number sample are arranged into replicates; each replicate is a national probability sample itself. The sample is released and controlled by replicate. [A replicate is a methodologically organized subsample which is geographically representative of the total sample of which it is a part.]

These procedures produced a national probability sample and data which were projectable to the population of white women in the contiguous United States whose households had telephone service.

This survey was conducted in 1989 using a national probability sample constructed from 1980 decennial census data. One might ask why 1980 data were used rather than waiting and having the sample constructed from 1990 decennial census data. The fact of the matter is that decennial census data are often slow in being made available to the public, as exemplified by numerous 1980 housing, population, and urbanization reports that were not published until 1983. Certainly, unpublished data were obtainable earlier directly from the Census Bureau, but with the time necessary to integrate this information into a sampling program, waiting for 1990 decennial census data would still have meant a delay of several years. Although the construction of the sample was based on the 1980 census, the important point to make is that the data compiled from the survey itself were in fact 1989 public opinion.

THE NATIONAL PROBABILITY SAMPLE
as acquired by Opinion Research Corporation

— 444 WHITE WOMEN —

Subsample Groups	Subsample Sizes
AGE	
18-24	36
25-34	106
35-44	90
45-54	73
55-64	60
65+	74
EDUCATION	
Incomplete High School or Less	38
High School Graduate	165
Incomplete College	115
College Graduate	125
OCCUPATION	
Professional/Manager/Owner	128
White Collar — Sales/Clerical	76
Blue Collar	49
Other (not included in the tabulations for OCCUPATION)	16
Not Employed	174
MARITAL STATUS	
Married	275
Not Married	169
GEOGRAPHIC REGION	
Northeast	91
North Central	113
South	148
West	92
METRO SIZE	
Non-Metro	145
Under One Million	141
One Million or Over	158

AGE, EDUCATION, and OCCUPATION each do not add up to 444 because respondents did not provide data.

Opinion Research Corporation's Telephone Caravan Sample consists of 500 women. Inasmuch as this study was limited exclusively to white women, fifty-six nonwhite women were obtained in the sample but not surveyed.

DEMOGRAPHIC TERMS

Occupation

Professional/Manager/Owner — Executives, Professionals, Technical and Kindred Workers, Managers, Officials, and Proprietors

White Collar - Sales/Clerical — Clerical, Office and Secretarial Workers, and Sales Agents and Workers

Blue Collar — Craftsmen, Foremen, Kindred Workers, Maintenance Repairmen, Carpenters, Plumbers and Electricians; Operatives and Kindred Workers, Apprentices, Laborers (except Mine), and Assembly Line Workers; Housekeepers in Private Household, Institutional and Public, Police, Security Guards, Beauticians and Barbers

Geographic Region

Northeast — Maine, New Hampshire, Vermont, Massachusetts, Rhode Island, Connecticut, New York, New Jersey, Pennsylvania

North Central — Ohio, Indiana, Illinois, Michigan, Wisconsin, Minnesota, Iowa, Missouri, North Dakota, South Dakota, Nebraska, Kansas

South — Delaware, Maryland, District of Columbia, Virginia, West Virginia, North Carolina, South Carolina, Georgia, Florida, Kentucky, Tennessee, Alabama, Mississippi, Arkansas, Louisiana, Oklahoma, Texas

West — Montana, Idaho, Wyoming, Colorado, New Mexico, Arizona, Utah, Nevada, Washington, Oregon, California

Metro Size

Non-Metro	under 50,000 population, not in a metropolitan area
Metro — 50,000 - 999,999	places in a standard metropolitan statistical area of 50,000 - 999,999 population
Metro — 1,000,000 or over	places in a standard metropolitan statistical area of 1,000,000 or more population

All demographic terms that have not been defined are to be taken as self-explanatory.

Opinion Research Corporation uses "Married" to mean married or living as married, and "Not Married" to mean single and never been married, divorced, separated, or widowed.

The idea behind this public opinion survey was to obtain data about current beliefs in the thinking of white women on various issues pertaining to interracial sexuality in America. Ten belief statements designed by the author were presented, each addressing a particular aspect of this complex subject. As will be seen, the term "Afro-American" rather than "black" has been used in the survey. Inasmuch as the first belief statement dealt with the word "black" as both a racial designator *and* a color term, "Afro-American" was utilized throughout the remainder of the survey so as not to confuse or unnecessarily influence respondents.

The women were asked to respond to each belief statement with one of four possible choices: "Strongly Agree," "Agree," "Disagree," or "Strongly Disagree." Although "No Response" was not one of the choices given by the interviewers, it was so recorded when a woman had no answer. In assessing the data obtained, "Strongly Agree" and "Agree" responses have been combined together and only one aggregate figure for agreement will be discussed. Likewise, "Disagree" and "Strongly Disagree" have been treated in the same manner. The tabulation charts at the end of Chapter 2 may be consulted to see the separate figures for each one of these four responses.

In order for readers to competently interpret the survey findings, an explanation of *sampling error* is necessary. Sampling error is statistically calculated from standard formulas as plus or minus a certain number of percentage points and shows a range or *tolerance* within which a result could be expected to fall if the interviews were repeated using the same procedures. Let us say, for example, that the sample of 444 white women responded with "Agree" to one of the belief statements at the rate of 74% and you wanted to know what tolerance range that percentage fell within. As can be seen in the table of sampling errors on the next page, 74%, the original percentage obtained, is subject to a sampling error of plus or minus 4 percentage points so the results could have fallen anywhere within a tolerance range of 70% to 78%. At a 95 in 100 confidence level, if the survey were to be repeated 100 times using the same sample size and the same survey design, 95 of those times the results would still fall within the same range of 70% to 78%.

In addition to examining the survey findings for the national probability sample of 444 white women, the results obtained from subsamples will also be looked at. It is to be noted that those 18-24 years old, those whose education was incomplete high school or less, the blue collar workers, and some of the other groups had much smaller sample sizes with much larger sampling tolerances, and therefore the findings for these groups must be viewed accordingly. Of course, the total sample of 444 gives the survey results with the smallest tolerance ranges.

Twenty-three different subsamples were examined in this study. Those that were numerically close to one another have virtually the same sampling errors, making it unnecessary to list each individually in the table below. The approximate subsample sizes given will adequately serve as points of reference.

Sampling Errors in Percentage Points (rounded off to the nearest whole number) at 95 in 100 confidence level

Survey Percentages Near	Sample and Approximate Subsample Sizes					
	444	275	150	100	75	50
10%	3	4	5	6	7	8
20%	4	5	7	8	9	11
30%	4	6	7	9	11	13
40%	5	6	8	10	11	14
50%	5	6	8	10	12	14
60%	5	6	8	10	11	14
70%	4	6	7	9	11	13
80%	4	5	7	8	9	11
90%	3	4	5	6	7	8

2

THE SURVEY

Here is the survey and its introduction just as administered by the interviewer. If you wish, take the survey yourself and compare your own responses with those of the national sample.

> Next we have ten statements dealing with sociology. This survey is being conducted for Dr. Lawrence R. Tenzer, affiliated with the American Sociological Association. I'm going to ask you for your own beliefs regarding interracial sexuality in America today, a subject which you may know little or nothing about. Please understand that we are not asking for your knowledge, we are only asking for your opinion. To what extent do you agree or disagree with each of the following statements:

1. I believe that the word "black," when used to refer to an Afro-American man as a black man, is perfectly acceptable, even though the word "black" as used in the English language, often has negative connotations.

    Strongly Agree   Agree   Disagree   Strongly Disagree

2. I believe that there has been a long and involved history of legal prohibition against interracial sexual relations.

    Strongly Agree   Agree   Disagree   Strongly Disagree

3. I believe that many more white men than white women have had interracial sexual relations.

    Strongly Agree   Agree   Disagree   Strongly Disagree

4.   I believe that the sexuality of an average white man is somehow different than that of an average Afro-American man.

   Strongly Agree   Agree   Disagree   Strongly Disagree

5.   I believe that many white men view their own sexuality as being somehow different than that of Afro-American men.

   Strongly Agree   Agree   Disagree   Strongly Disagree

6.   I believe that a white woman and a light-complexioned Afro-American man could have a child with a darker complexion than the man.

   Strongly Agree   Agree   Disagree   Strongly Disagree

7.   I believe that many white women have fantasized about a sexual experience with an Afro-American man.

   Strongly Agree   Agree   Disagree   Strongly Disagree

8.   I believe that if there were no social pressures against it, a white woman would date an Afro-American man if she wanted to.

   Strongly Agree   Agree   Disagree   Strongly Disagree

9.   I believe that the lack of acceptance of interracial sexual relations is at the root of racial prejudice in America today.

   Strongly Agree   Agree   Disagree   Strongly Disagree

10.   I believe that in the field of sexuality, interracial sexuality is a very worthwhile subject for future research.

   Strongly Agree   Agree   Disagree   Strongly Disagree

WHAT WHITE WOMEN BELIEVE

Perhaps the most outstanding and fascinating findings of this study had to do with Belief Statements 4 and 5. *The lowest agreement rate in the entire survey* was 17%, and this figure is found in the responses to Belief Statement 4 about whether white women believe the sexuality of an average white man is somehow different than that of an average Afro-American man. This finding in and of itself is of great interest, however, it really takes on an added dimension when compared with the 41% agreement rate for Belief Statement 5, which addressed whether white women believe many white men view their own sexuality as being somehow different than that of Afro-American men. These two perspectives on the issue of male sexuality yielded *very different* response rates. In light of these findings, one may ask, "What messages are white women picking up from white men that could possibly account for this difference?"

Belief Statement 6 regarding skin color inheritance had an agreement rate of 63% for all white women surveyed and one of the lowest disagreement rates at only 12%. This is exceptionally noteworthy for the simple reason that a white woman and a light-complexioned Afro-American man *can not* have a child with a darker complexion than the man. Despite popular belief to the contrary, this is a genetic impossibility. Skin color is not inherited in the same way as eye color is, for example, and this will be explained in the commentaries of Part Two.

The results of Belief Statement 7 showed a 27% agreement rate regarding the belief that many white women have fantasized about a sexual experience with an Afro-American man. The operant word here is "many." Although 27% is not a very large percentage in and of itself, one can speculate that a higher agreement rate might have been obtained had the word "some" been used instead of "many."

Belief Statement 8 had 65% of the white women in the national sample agreeing with the belief that if there were no social pressures against it, a white woman would date an Afro-American man if she wanted to. This finding speaks volumes for the tremendous influence being exerted on women today, inasmuch as the issue here is not one of *necessarily* dating Afro-American men, but rather, the *choice* to do so.

The responses of the white women surveyed appeared to be somewhat comparable in agreement (43%) and disagreement (40%) regarding Belief Statement 9, the belief that the lack of acceptance of interracial sexual relations is at the root of racial prejudice in America today. As will be seen, racial prejudice per se did not exist in the ancient worlds of Greece and Rome where interracial sexual relations occurred without prohibition. The issue of sex and race in America, however, has been and continues to be a controversial one as these two response rates illustrate.

The survey findings for Belief Statement 10 showed a 47% agreement rate regarding the belief that in the field of sexuality, interracial sexuality is a very worthwhile subject for future research. The operant word in this statement is "very." It is interesting to speculate whether the statement reading "a worthwhile subject" rather than "a very worthwhile subject" would have shown any significant increase in the agreement rate. Be that as it may, the fact remains that nearly half of the white women surveyed in the national probability sample agreed with the statement as worded.

Belief Statements 4 through 10 which have just been addressed deal with some of the more sensitive issues involved in interracial sexuality. The survey findings obtained for these seven statements are of particular interest because of the controversial nature of the material being considered. Belief Statements 1 through 3 which follow are certainly of interest also, however, their subject matter is less sensitive and more matter-of-fact.

The highest overall agreement rate for any of the ten survey statements was 77%, and this was in response to Belief Statement 1 regarding the word "black" being perfectly acceptable as a racial term even though the word "black" as used in the English language often has negative connotations. The no response rate was one of the lowest at 14% as was the disagreement rate at only 9%. Although Belief Statement 1 really has nothing to do with interracial sexuality per se, it *is* a statement in which white women were asked about black men. With this thought in mind along with the fact that black is both a color and a racial term, it is evident that the beliefs white women have about the word black were worthy of inquiry. Moreover, interracial sexuality is a subject that has never before been publicly surveyed in depth, and therefore it was decided that in order to help put respondents at ease, the first statement to be addressed in the survey should not have an overt sexual quality.

Belief Statement 2 was concerned with the belief that there has been a long and involved history of legal prohibition against interracial sexual relations, and here the agreement rate was 64%. This response indicates that many of the white women surveyed were familiar with the issue. The fact is that the first prohibitive law appeared on the books over 300 years ago.

Belief Statement 3 about whether many more white men than white women have had interracial sexual relations had rates of agreement, disagreement, and no response at 37%, 33% and 31% respectively. These rates were among the most evenly distributed for any statement in the survey. Based on these findings, it may be said that many white women were unaware of this aspect of American history.

Only the survey findings for the total sample of 444 white women have been discussed here because it is the total sample which gives the best overall composite picture on a national scale of what white women in America currently believe concerning the subject of interracial sexuality. In addition to the total sample, data was also tabulated for age, occupation, marital status, education, geographic region, and metro size. The subsample groups within each of these classifications, particularly some of the smaller ones, offer interesting comparisons if not often contrary viewpoints. Inasmuch as these groups have larger sampling errors than those of the total sample, they were not included as part of this overview but will be discussed in the demographic summaries to follow.

DEMOGRAPHIC SUMMARIES

Age

Generally speaking, all age groups showed lower agreement rates for Belief Statement 4 than for Belief Statement 5, both of which addressed male sexuality from different perspectives. The 18-24 group and the 65 and over group showed contrasting responses regarding the belief that the sexuality of an average white man is somehow different than that of an average Afro-American man. Disagreement rates were 61% for the former and 26% for the latter compared to no response rates of 11% and 58% respectively. With reference to the belief white women have regarding many white men viewing their own sexuality as being somehow different than that of Afro-American men, those 18-24 agreed at 64% compared to the 55-64 group at 25%.

The belief about skin color inheritance had the youngest and the oldest groups thinking along the same lines with agreement rates of 56% and 52% respectively. Belief Statement 6 showed some low disagreement rates among several age groups at 9% for those 25-34, 10% for those 35-44, and 7% for those 45-54.

Belief Statement 9 addressed the notion that the lack of acceptance of interracial sexual relations is at the root of racial prejudice in America today, and the major difference here showed up in the youngest and the older groups with those 18-24 more likely to be in agreement than those 55 and over.

Belief Statement 3 dealt with whether more white men than white women have had interracial sexual relations, and again the youngest age group differed from those 65 and over. This time the difference was in disagreement rates, the former at 56% and the latter at 14%.

Perhaps the one outstanding finding among the various age groups was that overall, those 18-24 and those 65 and over showed the most disparity in many of their responses.

Occupation

At face value, the similarities noted in the findings for each of the four groups appear to indicate that employment status was not a factor affecting responses.

The survey results for Belief Statements 4 and 5 showed that all four groups had a relatively low agreement rate for the former and a substantially higher agreement rate for the latter.

The blue collar group had a somewhat high rate of agreement at 41% regarding the belief about interracial sexual fantasy.

Over 50% of the women in each of the four groups agreed with Belief Statement 8 about interracial dating.

The professional/manager/owner group and the white collar — sales/clerical group showed similar patterns in their responses to Belief Statements 4, 5, 7, 8 and 9.

Marital Status

A majority of the women who were surveyed agreed with Belief Statements 1, 2, 6 and 8 regardless of their marital status.

Sampling tolerance notwithstanding, the agreement figures obtained for the belief about interracial sexual fantasy are worth a second look. With this one exception, those who were married as well as those who were not married appeared to show very similar ranges of agreement throughout the entire survey.

Overall, marital status did not appear to be a factor influencing a woman's beliefs about interracial sexuality.

Education

Responses to the two survey statements about male sexuality indicated some differences in opinion. Belief Statement 4 showed that those with an incomplete high school education or less disagreed at 24% whereas the college graduates disagreed at 58%. Belief Statement 5 had incomplete high school or less in agreement at 16% and incomplete college agreeing at 50%.

Of those women surveyed who were college graduates, 71% agreed with Belief Statement 6. Even to this educated group a false notion seems to prevail regarding how skin color is inherited.

Belief Statement 7 concerned with the belief that many white women have fantasized about a sexual experience with an Afro-American man showed strikingly different disagreement rates at 10% for the incomplete high school education or less group and 47% for the college graduates.

All of the education groups responded to Belief Statement 8 about interracial dating with higher agreement than disagreement. Worth noting is the 77% agreement rate for those women with some college education.

In the responses to Belief Statement 1 concerned with the word "black," the incomplete high school education or less group showed a relatively low agreement rate of 55%.

Belief Statement 2 addressed the belief that there has been a long and involved history of legal prohibitions against interracial sexual relations, and here the survey results indicated that the three groups with complete high school education or more had much greater agreement rates than the incomplete high school or less group.

At face value, the overall finding among the various education groups appears to be that those women with an incomplete high school education or less often responded contrarily to women who had obtained an educational level of high school graduate or more.

Geographic Region

All geographic regions with the exception of the Northeast showed considerably different agreement for Belief Statements 4 and 5. The figures obtained were as follows: Northeast - 22% and 36%, North Central - 17% and 44%, South - 17% and 42%, West - 10% and 43%.

The agreement rates for the belief about interracial dating are worth noting. The South agreed at 52%, the Northeast at 70%, the North Central at 73%, and the West at 74%.

Belief Statement 10 about interracial sexuality being a very worthwhile subject for future research showed interesting preliminary findings with the South in agreement at 38% and the Northeast in agreement at 58%.

Metro Size

The non-metro group and both metro groups all showed somewhat high agreement rates for Belief Statements 1, 2, 6 and 8. Especially interesting is the fact that a majority of the women in each of these groups agreed with the belief about interracial dating.

All of the metro sizes showed agreement rates significantly lower for Belief Statement 4 than for Belief Statement 5 with figures for the non-metro group at 11% and 38%, the metro group under one million at 22% and 43%, and the metro group one million or over at 17% and 43%. Also worth noting is the 50% no response rate for Belief Statement 4 given by the non-metro group.

In general, the agreement rates obtained for all three groups closely paralleled the responses obtained from the total sample of white women who were surveyed.

Belief Statement 1

I believe that the word "black," when used to refer to an Afro-American man as a black man, is perfectly acceptable, even though the word "black" as used in the English language, often has negative connotations.

	Strongly Agree	Agree	Disagree	Strongly Disagree	No Response
TOTAL 444					
White Women	10%	67%	7%	2%	14%
Age					
18-24	11%	69%	6%	6%	8%
25-34	13%	73%	8%	0	6%
35-44	14%	71%	4%	1%	9%
45-54	7%	63%	8%	7%	15%
55-64	7%	67%	8%	0	18%
65 and over	7%	58%	5%	0	30%
Occupation					
Professional/ Manager/Owner	13%	70%	7%	2%	8%
White Collar- Sales/Clerical	12%	74%	7%	0	8%
Blue Collar	4%	63%	10%	4%	18%
Not Employed	9%	64%	6%	1%	19%
Marital Status					
Married	10%	68%	8%	2%	12%
Not Married	11%	66%	4%	2%	17%

Belief Statement 1
(continued)

	Strongly Agree	Agree	Disagree	Strongly Disagree	No Response
Education					
Incomplete High School or Less	8%	47%	0	0	45%
High School Graduate	7%	70%	7%	1%	15%
Incomplete College	15%	67%	10%	1%	8%
College Graduate	10%	70%	6%	4%	9%
Geographic Region					
Northeast	11%	69%	3%	2%	14%
North Central	12%	65%	8%	2%	13%
South	8%	64%	9%	1%	18%
West	11%	73%	5%	2%	9%
Metro Size					
Non-Metropolitan	6%	71%	6%	2%	14%
Metropolitan Under One Million	15%	58%	9%	1%	17%
Metropolitan One Million or Over	9%	72%	6%	2%	11%

Belief Statement 2

I believe that there has been a long and involved history of legal prohibition against interracial sexual relations.

	Strongly Agree	Agree	Disagree	Strongly Disagree	No Response
TOTAL 444 White Women	13%	51%	14%	3%	20%
Age					
18-24	14%	53%	25%	0	8%
25-34	15%	55%	14%	4%	12%
35-44	18%	59%	8%	1%	14%
45-54	12%	56%	14%	1%	16%
55-64	7%	42%	17%	8%	27%
65 and over	8%	38%	11%	4%	39%
Occupation					
Professional/ Manager/Owner	15%	55%	12%	2%	16%
White Collar- Sales/Clerical	13%	55%	11%	4%	17%
Blue Collar	22%	47%	14%	4%	12%
Not Employed	8%	45%	16%	5%	26%
Marital Status					
Married	12%	53%	15%	3%	18%
Not Married	14%	47%	11%	5%	23%

Belief Statement 2
(continued)

	Strongly Agree	Agree	Disagree	Strongly Disagree	No Response
Education					
Incomplete High School or Less	11%	21%	21%	13%	34%
High School Graduate	8%	54%	15%	4%	20%
Incomplete College	20%	50%	11%	2%	17%
College Graduate	13%	56%	12%	2%	18%
Geographic Region					
Northeast	19%	52%	12%	1%	16%
North Central	11%	54%	13%	4%	18%
South	9%	46%	15%	5%	26%
West	15%	53%	13%	2%	16%
Metro Size					
Non-Metropolitan	10%	46%	16%	6%	21%
Metropolitan Under One Million	15%	49%	16%	4%	17%
Metropolitan One Million or Over	13%	56%	9%	1%	21%

Belief Statement 3

I believe that many more white men than white women have had interracial sexual relations.

	Strongly Agree	Agree	Disagree	Strongly Disagree	No Response
TOTAL					
444					
White Women	7%	30%	28%	5%	31%
Age					
18-24	6%	25%	53%	3%	14%
25-34	8%	24%	36%	6%	27%
35-44	6%	27%	37%	8%	23%
45-54	4%	37%	16%	3%	40%
55-64	8%	35%	22%	0	35%
65 and over	8%	35%	9%	5%	42%
Occupation					
Professional/ Manager/Owner	5%	26%	36%	6%	27%
White Collar- Sales/Clerical	9%	33%	33%	1%	24%
Blue Collar	8%	27%	37%	4%	24%
Not Employed	7%	31%	18%	4%	40%
Marital Status					
Married	7%	28%	29%	4%	32%
Not Married	7%	33%	25%	6%	30%

Belief Statement 3
(continued)

	Strongly Agree	Agree	Disagree	Strongly Disagree	No Response
Education					
Incomplete High School or Less	5%	24%	24%	0	47%
High School Graduate	6%	30%	33%	2%	28%
Incomplete College	8%	30%	25%	7%	30%
College Graduate	6%	31%	24%	6%	32%
Geographic Region					
Northeast	2%	35%	22%	9%	32%
North Central	7%	24%	34%	4%	32%
South	8%	32%	25%	2%	32%
West	8%	28%	30%	5%	28%
Metro Size					
Non-Metropolitan	6%	32%	26%	4%	31%
Metropolitan Under One Million	7%	26%	31%	8%	28%
Metropolitan One Million or Over	6%	32%	26%	2%	34%

Belief Statement 4

I believe that the sexuality of an average white man is somehow different than that of an average Afro-American man.

	Strongly Agree	Agree	Disagree	Strongly Disagree	No Response
TOTAL 444					
White Women	2%	15%	38%	8%	38%
Age					
18-24	6%	22%	53%	8%	11%
25-34	2%	19%	46%	6%	27%
35-44	2%	11%	40%	13%	33%
45-54	1%	14%	37%	7%	41%
55-64	0	10%	32%	7%	52%
65 and over	0	16%	22%	4%	58%
Occupation					
Professional/ Manager/Owner	2%	13%	45%	11%	30%
White Collar- Sales/Clerical	1%	12%	49%	7%	32%
Blue Collar	2%	14%	41%	4%	39%
Not Employed	1%	17%	27%	7%	48%
Marital Status					
Married	2%	15%	37%	8%	38%
Not Married	1%	16%	38%	8%	38%

Belief Statement 4
(continued)

	Strongly Agree	Agree	Disagree	Strongly Disagree	No Response
Education					
Incomplete High School or Less	3%	11%	24%	0	63%
High School Graduate	1%	19%	32%	4%	43%
Incomplete College	3%	15%	38%	14%	30%
College Graduate	1%	11%	49%	9%	30%
Geographic Region					
Northeast	2%	20%	29%	14%	35%
North Central	3%	14%	46%	5%	32%
South	1%	16%	31%	3%	48%
West	0	10%	47%	11%	33%
Metro Size					
Non-Metropolitan	1%	10%	34%	6%	50%
Metropolitan Under One Million	3%	19%	36%	7%	35%
Metropolitan One Million or Over	1%	16%	42%	10%	30%

Belief Statement 5

I believe that many white men view their own sexuality as being somehow different than that of Afro-American men.

	Strongly Agree	Agree	Disagree	Strongly Disagree	No Response
TOTAL					
444					
White Women	4%	37%	22%	2%	34%
Age					
18-24	3%	61%	11%	6%	19%
25-34	7%	41%	25%	2%	25%
35-44	4%	42%	27%	3%	23%
45-54	5%	36%	21%	3%	36%
55-64	2%	23%	25%	2%	48%
65 and over	3%	28%	16%	0	53%
Occupation					
Professional/ Manager/Owner	4%	42%	23%	6%	24%
White Collar- Sales/Clerical	1%	45%	22%	1%	30%
Blue Collar	10%	37%	24%	0	29%
Not Employed	5%	30%	20%	1%	45%
Marital Status					
Married	4%	37%	26%	2%	31%
Not Married	5%	38%	15%	3%	39%

Belief Statement 5
(continued)

	Strongly Agree	Agree	Disagree	Strongly Disagree	No Response
Education					
Incomplete High School or Less	3%	13%	16%	0	68%
High School Graduate	4%	39%	21%	1%	35%
Incomplete College	6%	44%	19%	4%	26%
College Graduate	3%	36%	29%	3%	29%
Geographic Region					
Northeast	5%	31%	22%	8%	34%
North Central	5%	39%	26%	1%	29%
South	2%	40%	18%	1%	40%
West	5%	38%	25%	1%	30%
Metro Size					
Non-Metropolitan	3%	35%	22%	0	39%
Metropolitan Under One Million	5%	38%	22%	2%	33%
Metropolitan One Million or Over	4%	39%	22%	4%	30%

Belief Statement 6

I believe that a white woman and a light-complexioned Afro-American man could have a child with a darker complexion than the man.

	Strongly Agree	Agree	Disagree	Strongly Disagree	No Response
TOTAL 444					
White Women	10%	53%	10%	2%	25%
Age					
18-24	6%	50%	31%	0	14%
25-34	13%	58%	7%	2%	20%
35-44	12%	59%	9%	1%	19%
45-54	12%	62%	7%	0	19%
55-64	3%	43%	10%	5%	38%
65 and over	9%	43%	8%	4%	35%
Occupation					
Professional/ Manager/Owner	10%	59%	9%	2%	20%
White Collar- Sales/Clerical	9%	58%	11%	1%	21%
Blue Collar	8%	51%	12%	0	29%
Not Employed	10%	48%	9%	3%	29%
Marital Status					
Married	10%	56%	8%	1%	25%
Not Married	11%	49%	13%	4%	24%

Belief Statement 6
(continued)

	Strongly Agree	Agree	Disagree	Strongly Disagree	No Response
Education					
Incomplete High School or Less	3%	34%	5%	13%	45%
High School Graduate	6%	57%	7%	0	30%
Incomplete College	17%	49%	14%	1%	20%
College Graduate	12%	59%	10%	2%	16%
Geographic Region					
Northeast	15%	51%	8%	2%	24%
North Central	10%	63%	10%	1%	17%
South	9%	47%	7%	4%	33%
West	8%	55%	15%	0	22%
Metro Size					
Non-Metropolitan	8%	55%	11%	2%	24%
Metropolitan Under One Million	11%	48%	11%	2%	28%
Metropolitan One Million or Over	11%	56%	8%	2%	23%

Belief Statement 7

I believe that many white women have fantasized about a sexual experience with an Afro-American man.

	Strongly Agree	Agree	Disagree	Strongly Disagree	No Response
TOTAL					
444					
White Women	4%	23%	32%	7%	34%
Age					
18-24	6%	36%	31%	8%	19%
25-34	4%	29%	36%	6%	25%
35-44	3%	24%	37%	6%	30%
45-54	4%	21%	38%	7%	30%
55-64	2%	13%	23%	12%	50%
65 and over	5%	16%	23%	9%	46%
Occupation					
Professional/ Manager/Owner	2%	26%	37%	7%	28%
White Collar- Sales/Clerical	3%	26%	38%	5%	28%
Blue Collar	8%	33%	22%	10%	27%
Not Employed	5%	16%	29%	9%	42%
Marital Status					
Married	4%	19%	36%	8%	34%
Not Married	4%	30%	25%	6%	34%

Belief Statement 7
(continued)

	Strongly Agree	Agree	Disagree	Strongly Disagree	No Response
Education					
Incomplete High School or Less	3%	24%	5%	5%	63%
High School Graduate	4%	25%	34%	8%	29%
Incomplete College	7%	22%	32%	5%	34%
College Graduate	2%	21%	37%	10%	31%
Geographic Region					
Northeast	7%	21%	35%	5%	32%
North Central	4%	20%	38%	7%	31%
South	1%	22%	27%	9%	40%
West	5%	29%	28%	7%	30%
Metro Size					
Non-Metropolitan	1%	21%	30%	10%	39%
Metropolitan Under One Million	6%	22%	30%	6%	35%
Metropolitan One Million or Over	4%	26%	35%	7%	28%

Belief Statement 8

I believe that if there were no social pressures against it, a white woman would date an Afro-American man if she wanted to.

	Strongly Agree	Agree	Disagree	Strongly Disagree	No Response
TOTAL					
444					
White Women	6%	59%	15%	3%	16%
Age					
18-24	11%	64%	14%	6%	6%
25-34	6%	67%	19%	2%	7%
35-44	6%	63%	13%	1%	17%
45-54	5%	56%	15%	5%	18%
55-64	8%	42%	20%	5%	25%
65 and over	4%	59%	11%	4%	22%
Occupation					
Professional/ Manager/Owner	9%	59%	15%	2%	15%
White Collar- Sales/Clerical	4%	66%	21%	1%	8%
Blue Collar	8%	61%	10%	4%	16%
Not Employed	5%	55%	15%	5%	20%
Marital Status					
Married	5%	61%	15%	4%	15%
Not Married	8%	56%	16%	3%	17%

Belief Statement 8
(continued)

Education	Strongly Agree	Agree	Disagree	Strongly Disagree	No Response
Incomplete High School or Less	5%	55%	3%	3%	34%
High School Graduate	5%	55%	19%	5%	16%
Incomplete College	9%	68%	14%	1%	9%
College Graduate	6%	59%	16%	4%	15%
Geographic Region					
Northeast	11%	59%	13%	2%	14%
North Central	3%	70%	13%	3%	12%
South	3%	49%	20%	6%	22%
West	10%	64%	12%	1%	13%
Metro Size					
Non-Metropolitan	3%	61%	13%	6%	17%
Metropolitan Under One Million	9%	59%	16%	3%	14%
Metropolitan One Million or Over	6%	59%	17%	1%	16%

Belief Statement 9

I believe that the lack of acceptance of interracial sexual relations is at the root of racial prejudice in America today.

	Strongly Agree	Agree	Disagree	Strongly Disagree	No Response
TOTAL					
444					
White Women	7%	36%	32%	8%	17%
Age					
18-24	8%	56%	22%	8%	6%
25-34	12%	42%	30%	7%	9%
35-44	10%	38%	34%	6%	12%
45-54	3%	32%	40%	8%	18%
55-64	2%	27%	38%	8%	25%
65 and over	4%	27%	27%	12%	30%
Occupation					
Professional/ Manager/Owner	7%	35%	38%	9%	11%
White Collar-Sales/Clerical	5%	36%	41%	7%	12%
Blue Collar	12%	39%	29%	4%	16%
Not Employed	6%	35%	26%	9%	24%
Marital Status					
Married	6%	37%	35%	6%	15%
Not Married	8%	33%	28%	11%	20%

Belief Statement 9
(continued)

	Strongly Agree	Agree	Disagree	Strongly Disagree	No Response
Education					
Incomplete High School or Less	5%	32%	21%	13%	29%
High School Graduate	5%	41%	32%	4%	18%
Incomplete College	10%	40%	28%	8%	14%
College Graduate	6%	26%	42%	11%	14%
Geographic Region					
Northeast	8%	31%	33%	9%	20%
North Central	6%	35%	33%	10%	16%
South	5%	38%	30%	9%	18%
West	11%	37%	36%	2%	14%
Metro Size					
Non-Metropolitan	6%	39%	27%	9%	19%
Metropolitan Under One Million	7%	37%	30%	10%	16%
Metropolitan One Million or Over	8%	31%	40%	5%	16%

Belief Statement 10

I believe that in the field of sexuality, interracial sexuality is a very worthwhile subject for future research.

	Strongly Agree	Agree	Disagree	Strongly Disagree	No Response
TOTAL					
444					
White Women	6%	41%	25%	7%	21%
Age					
18-24	6%	56%	19%	8%	11%
25-34	7%	48%	25%	6%	15%
35-44	7%	44%	28%	6%	16%
45-54	4%	32%	37%	10%	18%
55-64	7%	30%	20%	10%	33%
65 and over	5%	36%	20%	5%	32%
Occupation					
Professional/ Manager/Owner	5%	41%	30%	9%	16%
White Collar-Sales/Clerical	5%	51%	25%	3%	16%
Blue Collar	14%	39%	18%	6%	22%
Not Employed	5%	37%	22%	8%	27%
Marital Status					
Married	5%	40%	27%	7%	21%
Not Married	7%	43%	23%	7%	20%

Belief Statement 10
(continued)

	Strongly Agree	Agree	Disagree	Strongly Disagree	No Response
Education					
Incomplete High School or Less	5%	39%	5%	8%	42%
High School Graduate	4%	36%	28%	8%	23%
Incomplete College	10%	45%	22%	4%	18%
College Graduate	4%	45%	30%	7%	14%
Geographic Region					
Northeast	10%	48%	14%	8%	20%
North Central	5%	40%	31%	7%	17%
South	3%	35%	25%	9%	28%
West	8%	45%	29%	2%	16%
Metro Size					
Non-Metropolitan	3%	37%	30%	6%	24%
Metropolitan Under One Million	7%	44%	21%	9%	20%
Metropolitan One Million or Over	8%	42%	25%	6%	19%

PART TWO:

SELECT COMMENTARIES

Introduction to the Select Commentaries

The preceding public opinion survey has established that various beliefs about interracial sexuality do indeed exist among American white women at large. Now that these beliefs have been empirically confirmed, the next step is to account for their existence. Why might the American white women of today believe as they do? Where could these beliefs have come from? How have they been able to endure? The second part of this book provides perspectives on these questions and others by means of eight sociohistorical commentaries based on the subject matter of the survey statements in Part One. The issues to be considered include symbolism, different psychological phenomena, sexual misunderstandings, dating and marriage, and possibilities for future research. America's forgotten past will also be examined, "forgotten" because most books which describe the social history of America conveniently omit in-depth references to interracial sexual relations due to the controversial nature of the facts involved. When dealing with historical quotations, the punctuation, spelling, and capitalization have been modernized at the author's discretion where deemed necessary.

Each of the commentaries is followed by its own section of notes. These notes are comprised of bibliographic references for those who may want to verify information that has been presented or read more on a particular subject, and supplementary discussions which consist of important additional text designed to round out the understanding of certain issues.

Inasmuch as the term "Afro-American" was utilized in the belief statements of Part One, that term will be retained as a matter of consistency in any discussion of those statements here in Part Two. It is to be noted, however, that Afro-American, black, African American, Negro, and colored have all been used to designate persons of African descent, several being interchangeable throughout the course of American history and each somewhat in vogue at one time or another. In order to keep all of this terminology from becoming burdensome, terms have been used as their contexts dictate. For example, "Negro" has been utilized to preserve a historical flavor and at times also appears out of literary necessity. Wherever feasible, however, the currently popular term "black" was the one primarily used throughout the text. Unless stated or implied otherwise, black will be taken to mean black and mulatto together, that is, all persons with discernible African ancestry. Also, unless the context suggests otherwise, the term "mulatto" has been used in its general figurative sense to indicate a person with any degree of white and black admixture rather than its less frequently used literal sense meaning a person with one white parent and one black parent.

One last point must be called to the attention of the reader before these commentaries begin. Due to the sensitivities connected with discussions about interracial sexuality, information has been presented in a direct and factual manner with absolutely no intention to sensationalize or antagonize. The serious inquiry which you are about to read touches upon some very thought-provoking social and sexual issues. A mature attitude and an open mind are necessary when reading the Select Commentaries which follow.

3

THE COLOR BLACK - A DICHOTOMY?

A large percentage (77%) of white women in the national probability sample agreed with the belief that the word "black" is perfectly acceptable when used to refer to an Afro-American man as a black man, even though the word "black" as used in the English language often has negative connotations (Belief Statement 1). This finding appears to indicate that a clear distinction is being drawn between black, the racial term and black, the color term, a contrast entirely understandable in light of the fact that black people are not literally black (just as white people are not literally white).

The color black with its many negative connotations has had a long history spanning from Biblical days up through the present time. "Black" has been a referent to the devil, sin, filthiness, and ugliness – a strong contrast to the Puritan and Victorian legacy of "white" as a referent to God, virginity, purity, and beauty. The English language is structured in terms of black Mass, black magic, black sheep, blacklist, blackball, black eye, blackmail, black mark, black market. Many other examples could be cited which inculcate negativity with regard to the color black. We learn to fear black as the color of night, death, and the villain's hat and cape. We say that one's reputation has been blackened. Witchcraft and the black arts were condemned in Europe and colonial New England. The hearse is black. The widow's veil is black. But the color black has an opposite in the English language, and it is the color white. The bridal veil is white. To be "white as snow" is to be clean, innocent, or moral (as exemplified by the character Snow White). The President of the United States lives in the White House. To be "lily-white" is to be free of blemish or wrongdoing. In the game of chess, the white pieces move first. White lie and white knight have positive connotations as well. Certainly, blackberries, to be "in the black," and black tie have positive connotations, and the white shark, to be "white as a ghost," and whitewash have negative ones, but these anomalies and others are exceptions to the general semantic rule in the English language in which "white" connotes good and "black" bad. White and black are literally and figuratively opposites.

This conception of opposites holds true for other languages as well. Linguistic researchers Brent Berlin and Paul Kay investigated the universality and evolution of basic color terms by examining ninety-eight languages. They found that nine primitive languages in South India, the Congo, and New Guinea utilize only two color terms – white and black, the former used as an inclusive term for the color white and most light hues, and the latter used as an inclusive term for the color black and most dark hues. All of the other eighty-nine languages added additional colors on to the basic white and black. The figurative usages for the color white as good and the color black as bad appear to be virtually universal as well. Social anthropologist Frances M. Adams and linguistics specialist Charles E. Osgood tested high school students from twenty different countries regarding color concepts and found that all groups evaluated white more highly than black. Detailed work on the subject of color connotations has been done by social psychologist Charles Winick, who found black to be a disapproved color in many countries throughout the world. His data for the five African countries of Ethiopia, Nigeria, Sudan, Tunisia, and Union of South Africa show that all with the exception of Nigeria found black to be a disapproved color. *In all of these studies, it was the color black being addressed, not black as a racial term.*

What can possibly account for this virtual universality which designates white as good and black as bad? Aversion to the color black may be a natural and inevitable psychological phenomenon rooted in the fact that human beings are diurnal rather than nocturnal, that is, awake during daylight and asleep during darkness. Furthermore, nighttime is when we tend to have the frightening nightmares that we do not have in daydreams. Human beings from infancy onward grow up with anxiety about the dark because the security and control had in the visual world of daylight is not present at night. Daylight as the opposite of darkness is readily generalizable to white as the opposite of black.

Remarkably, by the time a child is of preschool age, the associations of white and black with good and bad have already been made. An important study was done by psychologists Cheryl A. Renninger and John E. Williams who found that white and black color connotations and white and black racial awarenesses both develop during the preschool ages of three to five years old. In other words, during the same period children come to understand the color black as bad, they hear Afro-Americans referred to as blacks and make the inevitable association. The noted child psychologist Jean Piaget calls this kind of reasoning "transduction." A=B; B=C; therefore A=C, proceeding from particular to particular in the absence of categories. From this line of thinking, "Black is bad,/ Black people are black,/ Black people are bad." If a child never undergoes an experience which questions this association, it is carried into adulthood unchallenged. When a child is still young and this association has not yet become permanent, however, it *can* be changed. Many responsible parents no doubt have clarified their children's thinking in this regard. Furthermore, educators should take note that a number of studies using puppets, black and white boxes, puzzles, color slides, and pictures have paired black objects with positive images and have influenced the thinking of preschool-age children about black people and the *association* between black and bad.

This whole idea of a young child unknowingly associating the color black with black people and badness is nothing new. The ancient Greek historian Agatharchides (fl. second century B.C.) wrote:

> The Negroes strike fear into the Greeks. Why? Is it because of their blackness or external features? This kind of fear does not last beyond the age of childhood. In wars and in the greater contributions, things are not judged by face or color, but by daring and strategy.

The fear of which Agatharchides speaks is that of xenophobia, not prejudice. Xenophobia, the fear of strangers or foreigners, is an instinctual component of survival whereas prejudice is a learned response.

———————

Up to this point the color black has been discussed rather

objectively and analytically in terms of fear and negativity, but another dimension exists as well, the dimension of fascination in which the color black is experienced subjectively and intuitively. Fear, negativity, and fascination are all beautifully and disquietingly intertwined in the human mind, so much so, that *symbols* are produced, those uniquely human creations generated by our unconscious. Here, a paradox which appears to contradict itself can exist without being resolved. Boundaries melt away so that we find ourselves at one in the same time both repelled by the fear and attracted by the fascination inherent in black as a color concept.

The depths of the ocean, the earth underground, and the darkness of night are three symbols which embody the fear/fascination paradox in the symbolic comprehension of the color black. The ocean holds fear in its infinite depths, and its depths are black. The ocean is uncontrollable, unfathomable, and is a symbolic as well as an actual tomb. Aside from fear, the ocean is also fascinating in its beauty and mystery. As the veritable womb of humanity, its darkness is inextricably bound up with procreation. Like the ocean, the earth is also a symbolic and actual tomb. For some the earth underground holds the fear of death, the final resting place for one's physical remains which are reclaimed in time. But the earth also supports life; the earth which we call Mother Earth literally holds the seeds of new life. Black top soil, the richest earth, provides the foundation from which procreation in nature takes place. The darkness of night envelops both the ocean and the earth. It also suggests something beyond fear to the human mind as symbol-maker. Darkness is the ultimate source. In the Bible darkness came first, then light. Darkness holds not only danger (that instinctual fear of night held by human beings as diurnal animals) but unimaginable distances and secrets, wonders as yet undiscovered and only dreamed of. The blackness of outer space holds the birth and death of stars. The darkness of night is a womb, the womb of the infinite universe and of all life in it. This womb exists in the microcosm as well, for the darkness of night is when humanity often concerns itself with its own procreation. It is indeed interesting to note that as *symbols,* the ocean, the earth, and nighttime with their darkness and blackness all seem to have one particularly fascinating aspect in common, and that is the regeneration of life.

In the final analysis, the color term black emerges as a dichotomy: black comprehended literally with its negative connotations as commonly used in the English language, and black comprehended symbolically with its positive associations of beauty, fascination, and procreation. *Of course, as a color term, black is separate and apart from the racial term which deals with people.* This distinction is a clear one.

Chapter 3.　THE COLOR BLACK - A DICHOTOMY?

Brent Berlin and Paul Kay, *Basic Color Terms: Their Universality and Evolution* (Los Angeles, 1969), 14-17, 22-25, 46-52. In the more advanced languages which they studied, red was the third color to evolve, followed by green, yellow, blue, brown, and then other colors. Frances M. Adams and Charles E. Osgood, "A Cross-Cultural Study of the Affective Meanings of Color," *Journal of Cross-Cultural Psychology* 4 (June 1973): 140; Charles Winick, "Taboo and Disapproved Colors and Symbols in Various Foreign Countries," *Journal of Social Psychology* 59 (April 1963): 363. Also, see John H. Franklin, ed., *Color and Race* (Boston, 1968).

Cheryl A. Renninger and John E. Williams, "Black-White Color Connotations and Racial Awareness in Preschool Children," *Perceptual and Motor Skills* 22 (June 1966): 771-85; Jean Piaget, *Play, Dreams and Imitation in Childhood,* trans. C. Gattegno and F. M. Hodgson (N. Y., 1962), 234.

There are numerous studies which address the modification of color and racial concepts in the thinking of young children. Among the more notable ones, see C. Drew Edwards and John E. Williams, "Generalization between Evaluative Words Associated with Racial Figures in Preschool Children," *Journal of Experimental Research in Personality* 4 (February 1970): 144-55; C. Allen McMurtry and John E. Williams, "Evaluation Dimension of the Affective Meaning System of the Preschool Child," *Developmental Psychology* 6 (March 1972): 238-46; Thomas S. Parish and Robert S. Fleetwood, "Amount of Conditioning and Subsequent Change in Racial Attitudes of Children," *Perceptual and Motor Skills* 40 (February 1975): 79-86; Thomas S. Parish, Robert S. Fleetwood, and Kingsley J. Lentz, "Effect of Neutral Conditioning on Racial Attitudes of Children," *Perceptual and Motor Skills* 40 (June 1975): 695-701; John E. Williams and C. Drew Edwards, "An Exploratory Study of the Modification of Color and Racial Concept Attitudes in Preschool Children," *Child Development* 40 (September 1969): 737-50. The general overview may be had in John E. Williams and J. Kenneth Morland, *Race, Color, and the Young Child* (Chapel Hill, 1976). Also, see Kenneth B. Clark, *Prejudice and Your Child,* 2d ed. (Middletown, Conn., 1988); Mary Ellen Goodman, *Race Awareness in Young Children,* 2d ed. (N. Y., 1964); *Interrace Magazine;*

Interracial Books for Children Bulletin, particularly vol.11, nos. 3 & 4, 1980; Francis Wardle, "Are You Sensitive to Interracial Children's Special Identity Needs?" *Young Children* 42 (January 1987): 53-59. The psychoanalytic perspective has been developed in Marjorie McDonald, *Not by the Color of Their Skin: The Impact of Racial Differences on the Child's Development* (N. Y., 1970).

Agatharchides *On the Erythraean Sea* 1.16, in *Geographi Graeci Minores,* ed. Karl Müller (Paris, 1882), 1:118. Xenophobic reactions begin in infancy. See Gordon W. Allport, *The Nature of Prejudice* (Cambridge, Mass., 1954), 130, 300-1; John W. M. Whiting and Irvin L. Child, *Child Training and Personality: A Cross-Cultural Study* (New Haven, 1953), chap. 12; Benjamin B. Wolman, *Children's Fears* (N. Y., 1978), 43-44.

In regard to racial prejudice being a learned response, many American history textbooks that were used in public schools during the 1930s and prior painted a degrading picture of post-Civil War blacks as being incompetent and worse, and it is easy to see how white Americans who studied this misrepresented history as children and young adults could have been affected by what they "learned." Furthermore, many of these students became parents and it is entirely reasonable to suggest that many instilled what they had learned about blacks into their own children who are today's middle-aged adults. It is indeed unfortunate that the prejudice learned in the public schools of the past is still having its influence felt. W. E. B. Du Bois, *Black Reconstruction in America* (1935; reprint, N. Y., 1969), 711-13 and 714-32 for additional discussion. For the South in particular, see Lawrence D. Reddick, "Racial Attitudes in American History Textbooks of the South," *Journal of Negro History* 19 (July 1934): 225-65. More current perspectives on the issue in general may be had in Louis L. Knowles and Kenneth Prewitt, eds., *Institutional Racism in America* (Englewood Cliffs, N. J., Spectrum Book, 1969), chap. 4, and Gerald Horne, ed., *Thinking and Rethinking U. S. History* (N. Y., 1988). Among many other instances of misrepresented history, see for example, Robert Eisler, *The Messiah Jesus and John the Baptist* (N. Y., 1931), chap. 15, and Hamilton Fish, *Tragic Deception: FDR and America's Involvement in World War II* (Old Greenwich, Conn., 1983).

For another discussion of symbolism and the color term black, see Howard E. Smith, Jr., *The Sensual Explorer* (N. Y., 1977), 177-78.

The use of the word black as a racial term has been the focus of an ongoing debate. Even today a controversy continues to exist within the black community itself regarding which designator is appropriate: Afro-American? black? African American? Negro? colored? A quick scan of the *Encyclopedia of Associations* shows that all of these terms are currently in use. If any were considered to be offensive, certainly the groups involved would have changed their names. The fact that these names have not been changed speaks for itself. Most recently, black seems to be the commonly used designator, but just as black replaced Negro, so too, the current popularity of black could wane. Should this occur, black could be replaced by any one of the other terms, or even by something entirely new for that matter. Looking at usage, it is interesting to note that Afro-American was popular along with Negro and continues to be so along with black.

4

SETTING THE SCENE -
HAVE ANY LEGAL PROHIBITIONS WORKED?

About two-thirds (64%) of the white women in the national probability sample agreed with the belief that there has been a long and involved history of legal prohibition against interracial sexual relations (Belief Statement 2). Indeed, such an actuality *has* been the case.

The story of interracial sex in America really began over in Europe long before the first colonist ever set foot on American soil. This can readily be seen in a number of European works of art and literature which address the subject of interracial sexuality. A brief survey of these fine arts will contribute to an understanding of what Europeans had been exposed to prior to their arrival in colonial America and will show that sex between whites and blacks in the thinking of many was really not a new idea.

The earliest extant literary work printed with movable type which deals with interracial sexuality is *The Novellino*, a collection of short stories by the Italian nobleman and courtier, Guardato Masuccio da Salerno. Although formally published in 1476, only about twenty years after the Gutenberg Bible, this work was read in manuscript form before that date. Most interesting is the fact that the tales appear to be fiction, but Masuccio states that they are all based on true stories. Interracial sexual relations between white women and black men appear in two of these fifteenth-century writings. In one, a woman is seen having sex with a Negro after verbally and physically seducing him, an act for which she becomes the object of scandal and excoriation; in the other, a beautiful but vain young woman who has compelled a Negro belonging to her father to have sex with her numerous times, finds herself tricked when a white male suitor paints himself black and appears as her lover.

Although Masuccio was widely read because the printing press made numerous copies of his work available, he was not the first to deal with interracial sex. The Italian writer Giovanni Boccaccio tells the story of one of the first interracial marriages, a Negro who married a white woman in the year 1345. An illustration of the wedding scene appeared in a fifteenth-century manuscript (PLATE 1).

The Dutch painter Hieronymus Bosch (1450?-1516) depicted interracial couples in his painting *The Garden of Earthly Delights* (PLATE 2). One detail presents a white woman and a black man afloat together in a small vessel, and a second shows a white man and a black woman sitting beside each other in a close and intimate manner (PLATE 3). *The Garden of Earthly Delights* with its unique qualities had much acceptance in its time and even appeared in the courts of Henry III of Nassau and Philip II of Spain.

William Shakespeare included the theme of interracial sexuality in two of his plays, *Titus Andronicus* (1594) and *Othello* (1604). In *Titus Andronicus* Aaron is a Negro who commits adultery with Tamora, a married white woman. Later in the play she gives birth to a mulatto child. In *Othello* a Moor (a North African tawny Moor although considered by many to be a Negro) marries Desdemona, the beautiful daughter of a Venetian senator. She is attracted to the noble and virtuous qualities of his character. Shakespeare patterned *Othello* after a story first published in 1565 by the Italian writer Giraldi Cinthio.

In the late seventeenth century interracial sexuality appeared again in English drama as a main theme in *Oroonoko* (1695), a play by Thomas Southerne which featured an African black man married to a European white woman. William Walker's play *Victorious Love* (1698) and John Hawkesworth's 1759 revision of Southerne both had to do with the same theme. Such interracial drama must have been extremely popular. The appeal of *Oroonoko* was characterized in statements made in 1702: "Oh! the Favourite of the Ladies. It had indeed uncommon Success." Literary historian Wylie Sypher has stated, "From 1696 to 1801, *Oroonoko* in one or another version was usually given at least once each season; no play, with the exception of *Jane Shore,* seems to have been more popular in the eighteenth century."

As a literary theme the black man married to the white woman also appeared in a few novels. Among the more notable of these were *Slavery; or, The Times* (1792) by Anna Maria Mackenzie,

PLATE 1

MARRIAGE OF PHILIPPA OF CATANIA TO
RAYMOND DE CAMPAGNE (in 1345)
Jean Fouquet's 1458 manuscript illustration
depicting one of the first interracial marriages

PLATE 2

Hieronymus Bosch
THE GARDEN OF EARTHLY DELIGHTS (early 1500s)
section from middle panel of triptych

PLATE 3

Details from THE GARDEN OF EARTHLY DELIGHTS
white woman/black man
white man/black woman

in which an African prince marries an English girl, and *Belinda* (1801) by Maria Edgeworth, wherein a Negro marries the daughter of an English farmer.

Plays and novels notwithstanding, interracial sexuality as a literary theme seems to have found its fullest expression in the medium of poetry. A series of popular English poems dealing with this subject began in 1646 with two love poems included in a literary anthology entitled, *The Academy of Complements.* One poem is from a black maiden to a white boy, and the other is his response. A year later John Cleveland published a similar poem. An excerpt reads:

"A Fair Nymph Scorning a Black Boy Courting Her"

> *Boy.* Our curl'd embraces shall delight
> to checker limbs with black and white.
> *Nymph.* Thy ink, my paper, make me guess,
> Our nuptial bed will prove a press;

In 1656 Abraham Wright incorporated the two poems from *The Academy of Complements* in his own anthology, and a year later Henry King and Eldred Revett included the same two poems in with their own original poetry. It is interesting to note that these poems with subject matter about black male/white female and white male/black female romantic relationships were published several different times and also appeared in manuscript form as well. They must have had a wide circulation. Also in 1656, John Collop published a collection of his poetry which included several poems about yellow (possibly mulatto) and black women. Excerpts read:

"Chymerica Poesis. On the Sight of a Yellow Skin'd Lady"

> What stranger agony's this? ah fire!
> Ah! lightning quickens my desire!
> . . . .
> Or is this Cupids yellow fire,
> Since every glance inflames desire?

"The Praise of a Yellow Skin; or An ELIZABETH in Gold"

> Thy yellow breasts are hills of fire
> To heat, not snow to quench desire.

"On an Ethiopian* Beauty, M.S."

Black specks for beauty spots white faces need:
How fair are you whose face is black indeed?
*[an archaic general term for Negro]

In the poem "The Praise of His Mistress," Collop seems to sum up: "The rainbow hath no colour I can't love." Edward Lord Herbert of Cherbury was yet another English poet who addressed the subject of interracial sexuality. His collection of poetry was first published in 1665 and included a poem entitled "The Brown Beauty" which speaks of a lovely mulatto woman named Phaie (Greek word for "dusky"). An excerpt reads:

> While the two contraries of Black and White,
> In the Brown Phaie are so well unite,
> That they no longer now seem opposite,
> Who doubts but love, hath this his colour chose,
> Since he therein doth both the extremes compose,
> And as within their proper center close?
> . . . .
> Phaie, your sex's honour, then so live,
> That when the world shall with contention strive
> To whom they would a chief perfection give,
> They might the controversy so decide,
> As quitting all extremes on either side,
> You more than any may be dignify'd.

Art is the symbolic representation of human experience. For contemporary art to be popular it must embody qualities which reflect the moods and values of the culture in which it is produced and consumed. Judging from the fine arts of Boccaccio, Masuccio, Bosch, Cinthio, Southerne, Shakespeare, the English poets and others, *interracial sexuality was a social and cultural reality in Europe long before the first English and other colonists came to America.* England had sizable populations of blacks beginning back in the latter sixteenth century, and although there is no record of the *extent* to which interracial sexual relations occurred, if art imitates life, such relations were certainly not unknown. It is interesting to note that intermarriage per se in English culture must have been considered a nonthreatening anomaly because it was not prohibited by law.

The social climate in America, however, appeared to be much less tolerant. Numbers of blacks were imported into the colonies for agricultural purposes which resulted in a black population larger than that back in England. Interracial sexual relations occurred to a greater extent and caused problems to arise, particularly in regard to the legal status of the mulatto children born of these unions. The Southern colonies of Virginia and Maryland were the first to pass legislation which attempted to regulate interracial fornication and marriage, and as will be seen, these early legal precedences had far-reaching effects. Massachusetts is also of particular interest because it was the only colony in New England to formally follow in the footsteps of the South. The laws of these three colonies will be examined in some detail in order to illustrate the *great extent* to which attempts were made to control interracial sex as colonial America developed.

The first blacks to land in the colonies were the "20. and odd" brought to Virginia in 1619. The exact number and location are uncertain. In September 1630, little more than a decade later, the first court case regarding interracial sex appeared. Here, the white man was whipped:

> Hugh Davis to be soundly whipped before an assembly of Negroes and others for abusing himself to the dishonor of God and shame of Christianity by defiling his body in lying with a Negro, which fault he is to acknowledge next sabbath day.

In October 1640 another case involving a white man and a black woman was recorded, only this time, it was the black woman who was whipped:

> Whereas Robert Sweat hath begotten with child a Negro woman servant belonging unto Lieutenant Sheppard, the court hath therefore ordered that the said Negro woman shall be whipped at the whipping post and the said Sweat

> shall tomorrow in the forenoon do public pen-
> ance for his offense at James city church in the
> time of divine service according to the laws of
> England in that case provided.

Such behavior was not uncommon and so many white men were impregnating black women that the legal status of their mulatto offspring became an issue. In 1662 Virginia passed formal legis-lation which resolved this question and in the process became the first colony to legally address interracial sexual relations between whites and blacks:

> Whereas some doubts have arisen whether
> children got by any Englishman upon a Negro
> woman should be slave or free, be it therefore
> enacted and declared by this present grand
> assembly, that all children borne in this country
> shall be held bond or free only according to the
> condition of the mother, and that if any Christian
> shall commit fornication with a Negro man or
> woman, he or she so offending shall pay double
> the fines imposed by the former act.

This was a very important law because it established the legal precedence of *partus sequitur ventrem,* that is, the child follows the social status of the mother. Under this jurisprudence, if the mother is a slave, the child will be the property of the slave's owner and will be considered a bastard because it has no legal father. What this law did very subtly was to provide the means for white men to be able to deny paternity and keep illegitimate interracial children with the status of their black mothers. On the other hand, white women having illegitimate interracial children were guilty at face value because the identity of the black father did not need to be established.

In order not to be found guilty of fornication, many whites, particularly white women, who were sexually involved with blacks sought to legitimize their relationships through formal marriage. The Virginia law of 1691 outlawed both interracial marriage in general and interracial fornication committed by white women on-ly. The provisions of this law give a sense for the kind of early legislation which dealt with the prohibition of interracial sexual relations in the colonies. Any free white man or white woman intermarrying with a Negro, mulatto, or Indian, bond or free, was banished from Virginia and had to be out of the colony within three months of the marriage. A free white woman who had an illegitimate child fathered by a Negro or a mulatto was fined fifteen pounds sterling or was sold into servitude* for five years if the fine could not be paid. If the woman involved was already a servant, she had to complete the term of her original bond and then was sold for an additional five year term. A particularly odious provision provided that whether or not a white woman was free, her mulatto offspring was bound into servitude by a local churchwarden until the age of thirty and then freed.

The Virginia laws of 1705 and 1753 retained the punishments of a fifteen pound fine or five years in servitude for white women, however, now their mulatto children were to be bound out by churchwardens until the age of thirty-one rather than thirty. (This additional year was probably to make up for a mother's lost time during pregnancy.) Incarceration was introduced whereby free white men and women intermarrying with Negroes or mulattoes, bond or free, were to be committed to prison for six months and fined ten pounds in "current money." Any minister performing such a marriage incurred the enormous fine of 10,000 pounds of tobacco.

In the 1691 and 1705 laws just discussed, the mulatto offspring of white women were bound in unconditional servitude. A law of 1723 extended this provision into the next generation. If such female mulatto servants themselves had any children while under bond, such progeny automatically became servants to the same master as their mothers for the same thirty or thirty-one year terms as their mothers originally incurred.

Of interest to note is that sex between whites and blacks occurred despite the relatively small numbers of the latter in the population of Virginia throughout the seventeenth century. It was estimated that

* People who wanted to come to the colonies but could not afford to pay for the sea voyage over often became indentured servants. Their transportation costs were paid in exchange for contracting to work a fixed number of years (usually between five and seven). Such work often included agriculture and field labors. The servitude of indentured servants was entered into voluntarily. Servitude, however, was also often involuntarily imposed by courts of law as a judicial punishment.

in the year 1648 there were about 15,000 whites and 300 blacks; in 1671 the approximate numbers were 38,000 whites and 2,000 blacks; and for 1681 the figures were put at between 70,000 and 80,000 people of whom 3,000 were blacks. Only afterwards by 1715 did the black population increase dramatically to about 23,000 with the white population at about 72,000. At any rate, there was always a shortage of white women in Virginia throughout the seventeenth century. Estimates vary, but the figures are one to two for every three white men. Edmund S. Morgan, a specialist in the history of colonial Virginia, states the case objectively and strikes at the heart of the matter: "Women were still scarce in Virginia in 1691....It would appear that black men were competing all too successfully for white women....By providing severe punishments for white women who gave themselves to blacks, the authorities...assisted white freemen to find wives."

As was the case in Virginia, the black population in early Maryland was not substantial either. The earliest figures available are those for 1707 at 29,226 whites and 4,657 blacks. Maryland also had a shortage of white women with figures for 1704 showing a ratio of about two to every three white men. Be that as it may, Maryland passed its first legislation dealing with interracial sex in 1664, only two years after Virginia's first law appeared. The language condemning women is strong:

> Freeborn English women forgetful of their free condition and to the disgrace of our nation do intermarry with Negro slaves...for deterring such freeborn women from such shameful matches, be it further enacted...that whatsoever freeborn woman shall intermarry with any slave...shall serve the master of such slave during the life of her husband and that all the issue of such freeborn women so married shall be slaves as their fathers were.

As in the later Virginia laws, this early Maryland law also included a specific provision regarding the offspring of such unions:

> And be it further enacted that all the issues of English or other freeborn women that have already married Negroes shall serve the masters

of their parents till they be thirty years of age
and no longer.

Instead of preventing interracial marriage, the Maryland law of 1664 inadvertently allowed masters to unscrupulously promote it. A master frequently owned white female servants and black slaves, and by encouraging or coercing them to marry, not only did the woman become his slave for life, but her offspring as well. So widespread was this abuse that in 1681 an act was legislated to rectify the situation. Despite the unethical and immoral behavior on the part of the masters, it was the women again (English as well as other white women) who were castigated in language even more severe than that used in the former act:

> Freeborn English or white women sometimes by
> the instigation, procurement, or connivance of
> their masters, mistress, or dames and always to
> the satisfaction of their lascivious and lustful
> desires, and to the disgrace not only of the
> English but also of many other Christian na-
> tions, do intermarry with Negroes and slaves...
> be it further enacted...the said woman servant so
> married shall be...made free instantly upon her
> intermarriage...and all children born of such
> freeborn women, so manumitted and free...as
> the women so married.

Whereas before such marriage resulted in the white female servant becoming a slave for life, she was now free with the master assuming the loss of any time remaining on her indenture. In addition a fine of 10,000 pounds of tobacco was exacted from the master for each offense, and the minister who performed the marriage ceremony also received the same fine.

The laws of 1664 and 1681 were concerned with white women and intermarriage. Legislation enacted in 1692 greatly enlarged the scope of the original laws to include other offenders, offenses, and punishments. Among other provisions, the mulatto children who were born to white mothers married to any Negro, free or slave, became servants themselves until the age of twenty-one. Those who were illegitimate served until the age of thirty-one. Another interesting addition appears in this 1692 legislation – white men are addressed in regard to sexual relations with black women:

> Any freeborn English or white man that shall...
> either intermarry with or beget with child any
> Negro woman or slave when proved against him
> shall be liable to the same pains and penalties...
> provided against English or white women.

As was the case in 1664 and 1681, this law also addresses "freeborn English or white women" and "the satisfaction of their lascivious and lustful desires," however, nothing is ever mentioned regarding the morality of "any freeborn English or white man." Furthermore, the provisions regarding white men were largely rhetorical because enforcement became a moot point. As was seen in the Virginia laws previously discussed, a Negro slave woman as owned property could have no *legal* father for her child, and in a claim by a free Negro woman, according to the wording of the law quoted above, the white man could only be punished in a case "proved against him." How could a free Negro woman *prove* paternity?

The Maryland laws of 1699, 1704, 1715 and 1717 all contained slight modifications but basically reaffirmed the interracial fornication and marriage provisions and penalties that were set forth in 1692. The law of 1728, however, specifically dealt with interracial combinations which had not been addressed previously. Free mulatto women having illegitimate children fathered by Negroes or other slaves, and free Negro women having illegitimate children fathered by white men each received a seven year term in servitude (as did white women) and their mulatto progeny became servants until the age of thirty-one.

The degree of disapproval which must have been felt toward interracial sex in the colonies of Virginia and Maryland can be seen in the severity of all of these laws. The Virginia fine of fifteen pounds is particularly notable in this regard because during the seventeenth century fifteen pounds was a considerable sum of money. The cost of transportation from England to the colonies, for example, generally ranged from five to six pounds, and in cases of clothing allotment and procurement commissions, between ten and twelve pounds. Furthermore, as was observed in the provisions of the Virginia laws discussed, servitude or incarceration were the penalties with no mention ever made of corporal punishment. Even so, it was not uncommon for white women who gave birth to illegitimate mulatto children to be brought to the county seat where they received a public whipping.

Perhaps most severe of all was the particularly inhumane punishment of selling the mulatto children of white women and black men into servitude. Virginia and Maryland were not the only colonies to institute this penalty. Along with provisions banning interracial sexual relations, the North Carolina laws of 1715 and 1741 and the Pennsylvania law of 1726 called for the mulatto children of white mothers to be sold into servitude until the age of thirty-one. The South Carolina law of 1717 drew a distinction between male and female children, the former bound out until twenty-one, the latter until eighteen. A later Virginia law of 1765 also legislated these same punishments. Delaware, however, had a change of heart. About seventy years after becoming law (1726/7?), the thirty-one year proviso was repealed in 1795, "whereas it is unjust and inhuman to punish the child for the offense of the parent."

Interracial sexual relations in colonial America favored white men from the very start. Beginning with the legislation of Virginia in 1662 which established the social status of the child as equal to that of its mother, white men forced their mulatto bastards back on their black slave mistresses who had no redress in terms of white paternity. Laws providing for sanctions against white men having sex with black women were for the most part cosmetic and unenforceable. The establishment of this jurisprudence throughout the colonies is all the more understandable in light of the fact that colonial legislatures were comprised entirely of white male law makers. The idea of interracial sexual relations was not new to these men inasmuch as many had undoubtedly been exposed to some of the interracial fine arts spoken of at the beginning of this chapter. Much of this art, particularly in the literature of Shakespeare, Southerne, and the English poets, continued to be produced and consumed throughout the eighteenth century during the same time the English colonies were establishing themselves. Furthermore, most of these white male law makers had been familiar with the antifeminist tradition and sexual double standard back in England. The result was inevitable. White men who had sexual relations with black women were socially tolerated; white women who had sexual relations with black men were treated "according to law." Not only did the sexual double standard exist in England and the colonies at the time these colonial laws were passed, twentieth-century historians have even treated the sexual behavior of white women and white men differently in their studies of this period.

As was true in the Southern colonies, interracial sexual relations also occurred in the Northern colonies, particularly in New England, despite the relatively small number of blacks there. Lorenzo Johnston Greene, an authority on the Negro in New England during the colonial period, states, "There was much sexual promiscuity among all races and classes in colonial New England, and no matter how carefully the authorities—civil and religious—strove to maintain proper sexual relationships, court records abound with cases of immorality." As a result of such interracial sexual relations, mulattoes must have been prevalent during the early colonial period inasmuch as Massachusetts (1693), Connecticut (1704), Rhode Island (1714), and New Hampshire (1714) recognized them in law as a well-defined class.

Of all the New England colonies, only Massachusetts passed legislation prohibiting sexual relations between whites and blacks. Of special significance is the fact that the Massachusetts law was legislated in 1705 at a time when there were very few blacks in the general population. In 1708 Joseph Dudley, governor of Massachusetts (1702-1715), reported that the number of blacks in the colony was only about 550, and in 1709 he cited an approximate figure for the entire population at "56,000 souls besides the blacks." What could have been responsible for the passage of such legislation in light of this disparity? The Massachusetts law of 1705 was entitled "AN ACT FOR THE BETTER PREVENTING OF A SPURIOUS AND MIXT ISSUE," so perhaps mulattoes threatened the caste structure, or maybe many were dependent wards of the colony. The punishments for interracial fornication and intermarriage included banishment, fines, and whipping. Even though the authority who performed such marriages received the enormous fine of fifty pounds, some must have still taken place because the Massachusetts law of 1786 added that "all such marriages shall be absolutely null and void." Worth noting, just four years later the federal census for 1790 listed 373,254 whites and *only* 5,463 blacks.

Slavery was abolished in Massachusetts in 1783, however, the law against interracial marriage remained in force. White women with mulatto children who wanted to legitimize their relationships through intermarriage as well as others sympathetic to the legalization of intermarriage sought to change the law. In 1839 a petition listing the names of over 1,300 women (no men) was submitted to the state legislature. It is most important to note that many of these women were married, and those who were not did not necessarily want to marry black men. They were all fighting for *the right of women to choose* to marry black men. Minot Thayer, a prominent politician who was against the legalization of intermarriage, headed a committee established to verify the authenticity of the signatures on the petition. Several errors were uncovered, and in an editorial proclamation added to their report, the Thayer committee stated that it was "inconsistent with the modesty of a virtuous woman to solicit the repeal of laws restraining the union of the white and black races in marriage." Maria W. Chapman, the leading female abolitionist in the state, renewed the effort for repeal and the 1840 legislative session was presented with petitions containing 5,032 female *and* 3,674 male signatures. This attempt was also defeated. After much politicking and heated debate, in 1843 the law against interracial marriage was finally repealed.

Massachusetts was certainly the exception to the rule regarding the fate of interracial marriage. The legacy of male domination left by the Virginia law of 1662 manifested itself throughout westward expansion and the pre-Civil War period. The laws banning sexual relations between whites and blacks which subsequently ensued were drafted by all male legislatures and were continued in the tradition of *partus sequitur ventrem,* the child following the social status of the mother. White men thereby retained sexual access to black women and at the same time perpetuated the double standard regarding white women.

The extent and scope of these later laws prohibiting interracial sex and marriage are illustrated by the following list (by no means complete) of states and years: Delaware - 1807, repealed in 1808, reenacted in 1829 and 1852; Louisiana - 1810, reenacted in 1825; Maine - 1821, 1847; Georgia - 1821, 1837 and 1859; Tennessee - 1822; Illinois - 1829; Indiana - 1829, 1843 and 1852; North Carolina - 1830, repealed in 1836, reenacted in 1838; Florida - 1832; Arkansas and Michigan - 1838; Iowa - 1840; California - 1850; Kansas and the Washington Territory - 1855; and Texas - 1857. At the conclusion of the Civil War in 1865, Alabama, Georgia, Mississippi, and South Carolina immediately addressed legislation dealing with interracial sexual relations.

In 1865 and 1866 many Southern states enacted what became known as "Black Codes," harsh legislation which deprived blacks of their civil rights much as the antebellum slave codes did. Many of these laws punished blacks more severely than whites for the same offenses. In response Congress passed the Civil Rights Act of 1866 which became the basis for the Fourteenth Amendment to the Constitution. Alabama, Arkansas, Florida, Georgia, Louisiana, Mississippi, North Carolina, South Carolina, Texas, and Virginia initially refused to ratify this amendment and were consequently denied representation in Congress.

The first section of the Fourteenth Amendment to the Constitution reads as follows:

> SECTION 1. All persons born or naturalized in the United States, and subject to the jurisdiction thereof, are citizens of the United States and of the State wherein they reside. No State shall make or enforce any law which shall abridge the privileges or immunities of citizens of the United States; nor shall any State deprive any person of life, liberty, or property, without due process of law; nor deny to any person within its jurisdiction the equal protection of the laws.

At first glance, it would appear that if blacks could enter into contracts, they could legally enter into the contract of marriage. Yet, in interpreting the provisions of the Civil Rights Act of 1866 and the Fourteenth Amendment, notable court decisions held that marriage was a States' rights issue and not a contract subject to federal regulation. Upon what was such an interpretation based? When the Civil Rights Act was deliberated in the House of Representatives, its final form was amended to omit any direct bearing on state segregation statutes because it was claimed that Congress lacked specific authority in this regard. Under the Fourteenth Amendment, this congressional hands-off sentiment concerning segregation issues set the tone for state court confirmation of state legislation regarding *miscegenation* (the formal term for all-inclusive interracial sex — fornication, adultery, marriage).

Once established to be constitutional by legal precedence, state laws banning miscegenation continued to be enacted and reenacted throughout the post-Civil War period and well into the 1900s. By 1950 twenty-nine states outlawed marriage between whites and blacks, fourteen between whites and Mongolians or Orientals, and five between whites and American Indians.

By the late 1940s social climate changed and allowed for a different interpretation. This change was exemplified in the national political party platforms of 1944 and 1948 which addressed America's intent to deal with discrimination effectively. In 1948 in the case of *Perez v. Sharp* (also known as *Perez v. Lippold*) involving a black man and a white woman, the Supreme Court of California held that the provision of the state's civil code which outlawed interracial marriage was in violation of the Fourteenth Amendment. In a four to three decision the State Supreme Court said,

> Marriage is thus something more than a civil contract subject to regulation by the state; it is a fundamental right of free men....There can be no prohibition of marriage except for an important social objective and by reasonable means.... Legislation infringing such rights must be based upon more than prejudice and must be free from oppressive discrimination to comply with the constitutional requirements of due process and equal protection of the laws.

This case was very significant because it set modern legal precedence.

In 1967 the United States Supreme Court ruled in the famous *Loving v. Virginia* case. Here, a white man and a black woman who were both residents of Virginia wanted to marry but were forbidden by law to do so. They went to Washington, D. C., were married there, and then returned to Virginia to live. As in *Perez v. Sharp,* the Supreme Court found the Virginia miscegenation law unconstitutional because it violated both the "equal protection" and "due process" clauses of the Fourteenth Amendment. In a unanimous decision the United States Supreme Court said,

> There can be no doubt that restricting the freedom to marry solely because of racial classifications violates the central meaning of the Equal Protection Clause....To deny this fundamental freedom on so unsupportable a basis as the racial classifications embodied in these statutes, classifications so directly subversive of the principle of equality at the heart of the Fourteenth Amendment, is surely to deprive all the state's citizens of liberty without due process of law.

At the time of the Virginia case, miscegenation laws were on the books of fifteen other states: Alabama, Arkansas, Delaware, Florida, Georgia, Kentucky, Louisiana, Mississippi, Missouri, North Carolina, Oklahoma, South Carolina, Tennessee, Texas, and West Virginia. In addition Alabama, Florida, Mississippi, North Carolina, South Carolina, and Tennessee all had miscegenation provisions *included as part of their state constitutions.* When the Supreme Court of the United States ruled the Virginia law against interracial marriage unconstitutional, in effect it did so for the other fifteen state laws and six state constitutions as well.

In conclusion, it can be said that there *has* been a long and involved 300 year history of legal prohibition against interracial sexual relations in America, a prohibition which began with the *colony* of Virginia in 1662 and ended after many a twist and turn with the *state* of Virginia in 1967.

Chapter 4.   SETTING THE SCENE -
              HAVE ANY LEGAL PROHIBITIONS WORKED?

On his writing being nonfiction Masuccio states, "The truth of which is approved by real and authentic events which have come to pass in former times, and in these our days." *The Novellino of Masuccio,* trans. W. G. Waters (London, 1903), 1:xiii-xviii, xxxii; 2:47-62 ("black moor," an archaic term for Negro, in originals). 1:5 for above quote.

For Boccaccio and Bosch, see Jean Devisse and Michel Mollat, *The Image of the Black in Western Art 2: From the Early Christian Era to the "Age of Discovery" part 2* (N.Y., 1979), 144, 240-42.

For years a controversy has been raging in the professional literature as to whether Othello was a North African tawny Moor or a Negro, a debate that has not been taken lightly. The issue is a complicated one, but it appears that Othello *is* a tawny Moor after all. For those readers who are especially knowledgeable concerning Shakespeare and his contemporaries, the arguments which follow are worth careful consideration. Other readers will understand that source materials have been identified but not developed because discussion here must be limited.

The geographical references in *Othello* 1.1.111-12 and 4.2.224 (all Shakespeare line numbers from *The Riverside Shakespeare*); the "marble" reference in 3.3.460-62 compared with John Leo, *A Geographical Historie of Africa,* trans. John Pory (1600; reprint, N. Y., 1969), 1:41; Othello's insane jealousy and Leo 1:40, 2:49; Bernard Harris, "A Portrait of a Moor," *Shakespeare Survey* 11 (1958): 89-97; *The Novellino* 2:22-33. Also, Thomas Heywood, *The Fair Maid of the West,* ed. Robert K. Turner, Jr. (Lincoln, Bison Book, 1967), compare 5.1.7-9 and 5.2.64-65 in part 1.

If indeed Shakespeare's Othello was patterned after Cinthio's Moor, then Othello is definitely a tawny Moor. This would be so because of the definitions for "Moro," "Ethiopo," and "Negro" given by William Thomas in his contemporary dictionary, *Principal Rules of the Italian Grammer.* Cinthio was a professor of medicine, philosophy, and belles-lettres at the University of Ferrara. Would he have used "Moro" in his writings if "Ethiopo" or "Negro" was meant? See editions of 1550, 1562, and 1567, pp. M2r, X2r, and X4r. (Cinthio's work was first published in 1565.)

Of course, it can also be argued that because the infidel was blackened in the visual arts, he was blackened in the dramatic arts as well, making Othello appear on stage with a literally black complexion (despite the fact that he is obviously a Christian). This theatrical device would also visually reinforce the verbal illusions to black and white which occur throughout the play. Even if true, which is probable, Othello would still be a tawny Moor and not a Negro. Regarding the origins of blackening, see Devisse and Mollat, *Image,* 18, 20-22, 37, 61, 71, 82-84.

Furthermore, among all of the epithets hurled at Othello, he is never called a "black Moor" as Aaron is in *Titus Andronicus* 3.2.78. Othello speaks of himself as being black, but these are figurative references as in *King Henry VI. Part 1* 1.2.84; *King Henry VI. Part 2* 3.2.168; *The Two Gentlemen of Verona* 4.4.156 and 5.2.10.

Shakespeare also uses the word "black" as an excoriation in *Love's Labor's Lost* 4.3.243-73 and in references to the Dark Lady of the sonnets who is a white woman. One physical attribute is discussed in Horace Davis, "The Comparison of Hair to Wires in Sonnet 130," *Critic* 19 (June 24, 1893): 419. Sharing a likeness with the Dark Lady in Sonnet 130 is the poem "To a black Gentlewoman Mistresse" by Abraham Wright, in *Parnassus Biceps or Several Choice Pieces of Poetry, 1656,* comp. A. Wright and ed. G. Thorn-Drury (London, 1927), 128, and 75-77 for another treatment. Also, Wright, *Parnassus,* 76 is like Leslie Hotson's discussion of the Dark Lady and Lucy Negro in *Mr. W. H.* (N. Y., 1965), 244-45. Perhaps her appellation is related to the "conscience" definition given by John Florio in *Queen Anna's New World of Words, Or Dictionarie of the Italian and English Tongues* (1611; reprint, Menston, Eng., 1968), 330. Florio's definition may also explain *The Merchant of Venice* 3.5.38-39 in light of the fact that tawny Moors are referred to as Negroes in *Lust's Dominion* and George Peele's *The Battle of Alcazar.* In addition, see Edward H. Sugden, *A Topographical Dictionary to the Works of Shakespeare and His Fellow Dramatists* (N. Y., 1969), 361.

More on *Oroonoko* may be had in John Wendell Dodds, *Thomas Southerne Dramatist* (Hamden, Conn., 1970), 128, 137, 153, 156, 158; [Charles Gildon], *A Comparison Between the Two Stages* (1702; reprint, N. Y., 1973), 30. Two pages later *Oroonoko* is referred to as a masterpiece. Wylie Sypher, *Guinea's Captive Kings: British Anti-Slavery of the XVIIIth Century* (Chapel Hill, 1942), 120-21, 287, quote on 116.

Regarding the novels, see Eva Beatrice Dykes, *The Negro in English Romantic Thought* (Washington, 1942), 135, 140, 145.

The poetic excerpts of Cleveland, Collop, and Lord Herbert have been partially modernized.

The Academy of Complements, 7th ed. (London, 1646), 191-92; *The Poems of John Cleveland,* ed. Brian Morris and Eleanor Withington (Oxford, 1967), 22-23; Wright, *Parnassus,* 90-91, 181; *The Poems of Henry King,* ed. Margaret Crum (Oxford, 1965), 151; Eldred Revett, *Selected Poems. Humane and Divine,* ed. Donald M. Friedman (Liverpool, 1966), 21-24, 39-40, and also 36-38. Much of this poetry was based on a Latin poem by George Herbert (published posthumously) which concerned itself with a white man and a black woman. *The Works of George Herbert,* ed. F. E. Hutchinson (Oxford, 1941), 437. Gerard Previn Meyer is in error when he states that the "Rainolds and King poems" did not appear in print before 1657. The fact is that both were included in the 1646 edition of *The Academy of Complements* cited above. "The Blackamoor and Her Love," *Philological Quarterly* 17 (October 1938): 373. These two poems have been erroneously attributed to Sir John Davies as noted by Robert Krueger, ed., *The Poems of Sir John Davies* (Oxford, 1975), 313 (unnumbered).

The Poems of John Collop, ed. Conrad Hilberry (Madison, 1962), 111-18; *The Poems English and Latin of Edward Lord Herbert of Cherbury,* ed. G. C. Moore Smith (Oxford, 1923), 60, 157. The internal evidence in "The Brown Beauty" shows Phaie to be a mulatto rather than a white woman.

Of additional interest here may be "ELEGIE XVII. Variety" lines 38-41 in *The Poems of John Donne,* ed. J. C. Grierson (London, 1966), 1:114.

For information on blacks in England, see James Walvin, *The Black Presence: A Documentary History of the Negro in England, 1555-1860* (N. Y., 1971).

Winthrop D. Jordan has done definitive work on white male racial attitudes in America from precolonial times up through the early nineteenth century. As for the intolerant social climate toward interracial sexual relations, see *White Over Black: American Attitudes Toward the Negro, 1550-1812* (Chapel Hill, 1968), especially chap. 4.

Regarding the "20. and odd," see Wesley Frank Craven, *White, Red, and Black: The Seventeenth-Century Virginian* (Charlottesville, 1971), 77-80. Davis and Sweat cited in Helen Tunnicliff Catterall, ed., *Judicial Cases Concerning American Slavery and the Negro* (1926; reprint, N. Y., 1968), 1:77, 78. Robert Sweat is described as a "gentleman" in a land patent he received from Virginia in 1628. Philip Alexander Bruce, *Economic History of Virginia in the Seventeenth Century* (1895; reprint, N. Y., 1935), 2:109.

William Waller Hening, ed., *The Statutes at Large; Being a Collection of All the Laws of Virginia* (N. Y., 1810-1823), 2:170 [1662]. The fine for fornication "imposed by the former act" was 500 pounds of tobacco, now doubled to 1,000 pounds for interracial fornication. See 2:115.

Regarding *partus sequitur ventrem,* see Bruce, *Economic History* 2:99-100; Wilbert E. Moore, "Slave Law and the Social Structure," *Journal of Negro History* 26 (April 1941): 185-86 and n. 32. Examples of antebellum expositions are in Thomas R. R. Cobb, *An Inquiry into the Law of Negro Slavery in the United States of America* (Phila., 1858), 68-69, and George M. Stroud, *A Sketch of the Laws Relating to Slavery,* 2d ed. (Phila., 1856), 16-21.

There were a few interesting exceptions to the *partus sequitur ventrem* policy worth noting. The Maryland law of 1664 provided that "all children born of any Negro or other slave shall be slaves as their fathers were for the term of their lives." In Connecticut in 1704, a mulatto sued for his freedom and won because "his father was a white man" even though his mother was a black slave. An example is also to be found in the records of the Superior Council of Louisiana for November 14, 1745: "Report on legal freedom. Vincent Le Porche files a statement to the intent that one Marie Louise is not a slave but should enjoy complete liberty, being the daughter of a Frenchman." William Hand Browne et al., eds., *Archives of Maryland* (Baltimore, 1883-), 1:533; William C. Fowler, "The Historical Status of the Negro in Connecticut," *Historical Magazine,* 3d ser., 3 (January 1874): 16; Heloise H. Cruzat, trans., "Records of the Superior Council of Louisiana, LII," *Louisiana Historical Quarterly* 14 (October 1931): 598.

Virginia laws are in Hening, *Statutes* 3:86-87 [1691], 453-54 [1705], 4:133 [1723], 6:361-62 [1753]. In the 1770 Virginia court case *Howell v. Netherland,* Thomas Jefferson represented a mulatto who was suing for his freedom. His grandmother "begotten on a white woman by a Negro man" was bound out for thirty-one years in accordance with the 1705 law and her child in turn (the plaintiff's mother) was equally bound out for the same term by the 1723 law. The court found that the plaintiff as grandchild could not be penalized and was free. Catterall, *Judicial Cases* 1:90-91.

Specific wording varied in population estimates for seventeenth-century Virginia: for 1648 – "15,000 English; 300 Negro servants," for 1671 – "40,000 persons, men, women, and children, of which 2,000 are black slaves," for 1681 – "70,000 or 80,000 population, of which...3,000 blacks." Evarts B. Greene and Virginia D. Harrington, *American Population Before the Federal Census of 1790* (1932; reprint, Gloucester, Mass., 1966), 136-37, 139. Regarding the shortage of white women, see Herbert Moller, "Sex Composition and Correlated Culture Patterns of Colonial America," *William and Mary Quarterly,* 3d ser., 2 (April 1945): 118. Edmund S. Morgan, *American Slavery/American Freedom: The Ordeal of Colonial Virginia* (N. Y., 1975), 336.

For Maryland population figures, see Greene and Harrington, *American Population,* 124, and Browne et al., *Archives of Maryland* 25:256 [1704]. The laws are cited in *Archives* 1:533-34 [1664] (sometimes incorrectly cited as 1661, 1662 or 1663), 7:204-5 [1681], 13:546-49 [1692], 22:552 [1699], 26:259-60 [1704], 30:289-90 [1715], 33:112 [1717], 36:275-76 [1728]. Catterall, *Judicial Cases* 4:2-3, 49-50, 52 for more on the law of 1681. This early Maryland legislation and its ramifications are discussed in Jonathan L. Alpert, "The Origins of Slavery in the United States - The Maryland Precedent," *American Journal of Legal History* 14 (July 1970): 189-221, and Whittington B. Johnson, "The Origin and Nature of African Slavery in Seventeenth Century Maryland," *Maryland Historical Magazine* 73 (September 1978): 236-45.

Transportation costs may be had in Lewis Cecil Gray, *History of Agriculture in the Southern United States to 1860* (1932; reprint, Gloucester, Mass., 1958), 1:365. For public whippings, see Bruce, *Economic History* 2:111.

In addition to the Virginia and Maryland legislation already cited which provided for the selling of mulatto children into servitude, see Walter Clark, ed., *The State Records of North Carolina* (Goldsboro, 1904), 23:65, 195; James T. Mitchell and Henry Flanders, comps., *The Statutes at Large of Pennsylvania from 1682 to 1801* (Harrisburg, 1897), 4:63; Thomas Cooper, ed., *The Statutes at Large of South Carolina* (Columbia, 1838), 3:20; Hening, *Statutes* 8:134-35; John D. Cushing, comp., *The First Laws of the State of Delaware* (Wilmington, 1981), 1:pt. 1, 108 and 2:pt. 2, 1201. The most likely date for the Delaware legislation (chap. 44, "An ACT against adultery and fornication") is 1726/7. John Codman Hurd's citation of 1721 is incorrect. *The Law of Freedom and Bondage in the United States* (1858; reprint, N. Y., 1968), 1:292.

William Goodell has commented on the vagueness which often characterized early colonial legislation. *Slavery and Anti-Slavery; A History of the Great Struggle in Both Hemispheres* (1852; reprint, N. Y., 1968), chap. 3.

Regarding the impact of white male favoritism shown in the early interracial legislation of Virginia, legal scholar A. Leon Higginbotham, Jr. states, "The law's greater sensitivity to interracial sexual activity and white male domination remained for centuries." *In the Matter of Color: Race and the American Legal Process, the Colonial Period* (N. Y., 1978), 40-47, quote on 41.

More on the antifeminist tradition in England may be had in Felicity A. Nussbaum, *The Brink of All We Hate: English Satires on Women, 1660-1750* (Lexington, Ky., 1984); Katherine M. Rogers, *The Troublesome Helpmate: A History of Misogyny in Literature* (Seattle, Washington Paperback, 1968), chap. 5 and her *Feminism in Eighteenth-Century England* (Urbana, 1982). Earlier references are cited in R. W. Dent, *Proverbial Language in English Drama Exclusive of Shakespeare, 1495-1616, an Index* (Berkeley, 1984), 745-53. For the sexual double standard in England, see Lawrence Stone, *The Family, Sex and Marriage in England, 1500-1800* (London, 1977), 501-7, 544-45. Historian Julia C. Spruill observes, "In the colonies as in the Mother Country, a gentleman's illicit affairs did not prevent his moving in the best society." *Women's Life and Work in the Southern Colonies* (N. Y., 1972), 172-77, quote on 174. Also, see Bruce, *Economic History* 2:110.

Several examples may be cited here of twentieth-century historians who have continued to perpetuate the sexual double standard. Lewis Cecil Gray writes that "many of the women were of the scum of English society." Regarding Maryland servants, Eugene Irving McCormac notes that "there were often women of a very low type." Philip Alexander Bruce, authority on the colony of Virginia in the seventeenth century, states, "The class of white women who were required to work in the fields belonged to the lowest rank in point of character...they yielded to the temptations of the situations in which they were placed." Many of these women may have had a low social status, but that is not necessarily to be confused with a low morality. Where are the statements about the low social status of the many white men who consorted with black women? Where are the statements addressing the morality of the white men involved in such relationships regardless of their social status? Gray, *History of Agriculture* 1:503; McCormac, *White Servitude in Maryland* (Baltimore, 1904), 67; Bruce, *Economic History* 2:112.

Lorenzo Johnston Greene, *The Negro in Colonial New England* (1942; reprint, N. Y., Atheneum, 1974), 202-10, 326, quote on 202. Besides fornication, some evidence suggests that formal intermarriages also took place. In Connecticut in 1763, two interracial marriages between black men and white women were recorded, however, earlier possible records may have been destroyed. Frederic W. Bailey, comp., *Early Connecticut Marriages as Found on Ancient Church Records Prior to 1800* (New Haven, 1896), 7-8. General references for this period are included in Laura Hutchison Hyde, "Negro Slavery in Colonial New England" (Master's thesis, Univ. of Chicago, 1914).

For Dudley's figures, see George H. Moore, *Notes on the History of Slavery in Massachusetts* (N. Y., 1866), 50, and Greene and Harrington, *American Population*, 14. The Massachusetts laws of 1705 and 1786 are cited in *The Acts and Resolves, Public and Private, of the Province of the Massachusetts Bay* (Boston, 1869), 1:578; *The Laws of the Commonwealth of Massachusetts from November 28, 1780...to February 28, 1807* (Boston, 1807), 323-24. For the census statistics, see J. D. B. DeBow, *Statistical View of the United States...A Compendium of the Seventh Census* (Washington, 1854), 45, 63.

The legal struggles over interracial marriage in Massachusetts are detailed in Louis Ruchames, "Race, Marriage, and Abolition in Massachusetts," *Journal of Negro History* 40 (July 1955): 256-69, quote on 262-63; Henry Wilson, *History of the Rise and Fall of the Slave Power in America,* 4th ed. (Boston, 1875), 1:chap. 34. Also, see Truman Nelson, ed., *Documents of Upheaval: Selections from*

William Lloyd Garrison's THE LIBERATOR, 1831-1865 (N. Y., 1966), 50-51. The 1843 law may be had in *Supplements to the Revised Statutes. Laws of the Commonwealth of Massachusetts, Passed Subsequently to the Revised Statutes: 1836-1849 Inclusive* (Boston, 1849), 248. Many of the women who fought to change the intermarriage law were abolitionists, individuals involved in the movement to abolish slavery. For a list of formal abolitionist principles, see Goodell, *Slavery and Anti-Slavery,* 398-99. The grass-roots perspective has been addressed in Edward Magdol, *The Antislavery Rank and File: A Social Profile of the Abolitionists' Constituency* (Westport, 1986). Unfortunately, critics of the abolitionists have often written them off as zealous fanatics. Although there were some abolitionists who were certainly extremists, it is incorrect to say that all or even most were.

Interracial marriage laws of the pre-Civil War period are cited in Hurd, *Law of Freedom and Bondage;* Franklin Johnson, *The Development of State Legislation Concerning the Free Negro* (1919; reprint, Westport, 1979); Charles S. Mangum, Jr., *The Legal Status of the Negro* (Chapel Hill, 1940); Gilbert T. Stephenson, *Race Distinctions in American Law* (N. Y., 1910).

For verbatim copies of the "Black Codes," the Civil Rights Act of 1866, and other relevant legislation of the period, see Edward McPherson, *The Political History of the United States of America During the Period of Reconstruction* (Washington, 1875); Walter L. Fleming, *Laws Relating to Freedmen, 1865-6* (Morgantown, W. Va., 1904) and his *Documentary History of Reconstruction,* 2 vols. bound as 1 (1906/7; reprint, Gloucester, Mass., 1960). Also, see Theodore Brantner Wilson, *The Black Codes of the South* (University, Al., 1965); Alfred H. Kelly and Winfred A. Harbison, *The American Constitution,* 3d ed. (N. Y., 1963), 457-70.

Regarding the Fourteenth Amendment and court decisions, see Mangum, *Legal Status,* 239 n. 9, 240 nn. 11, 12; "Intermarriage with Negroes - A Survey of State Statutes," *Yale Law Review* 36 (April 1927): 860 nn. 6, 7, 8; Cyrus E. Phillips, IV, "Miscegenation: The Courts and the Constitution," *William and Mary Law Review* 8 (Fall 1966): 135 n. 13; Stephenson, *Race Distinctions,* chap. 6. For the Fourteenth Amendment and miscegenation, see R. Carter Pittman, "The Fourteenth Amendment: Its Intended Effect on Anti-Miscegenation Laws," *North Carolina Law Review* 43 (December

1964): 92-109, and Alfred Avins, "Anti-Miscegenation Laws and the Fourteenth Amendment: The Original Intent," *Virginia Law Review* 52 (October 1966): 1224-55.

Congressional sentiment may have regarded miscegenation and other segregation issues as being States' rights, but the right to vote was a different matter. When many states denied voting rights to black men, Congress passed the Fifteenth Amendment in 1869 (ratified in 1870): "The right of citizens of the United States to vote shall not be denied or abridged by the United States or by any State on account of race, color, or previous condition of servitude." Despite the term "citizens," voting rights were still denied to black women as well as white women. It was not until the ratification of the Nineteenth Amendment in 1920 that *all* women were given the right to vote.

The large and diverse body of miscegenation laws legislated from the post-Civil War onward are addressed in Jack Greenberg, *Race Relations and American Law* (N. Y., 1959), 346-47 n. 22, 397-98; Johnson, *Development of State Legislation;* Mangum, *Legal Status;* Stephenson, *Race Distinctions.* Somewhat dated but still worthwhile is Pauli Murray, comp. and ed., *States' Laws on Race and Color* (n. p., 1950).

For the civil rights planks in the 1944 and 1948 national political party platforms, see Richard Bardolph, ed., *The Civil Rights Record: Black Americans and the Law, 1849-1970* (N. Y., 1970), 244-48. The leadership of President Harry S. Truman in the movement toward equality under law was exemplified in *To Secure These Rights: The Report of the President's Committee on Civil Rights* (Washington, 1947).

For quotes from *Perez v. Sharp* (under the name, *Perez v. Lippold*), see Lloyd H. Riley, "Miscegenation Statutes - A Reevaluation of Their Constitutionality in Light of Changing Social and Political Conditions," *Southern California Law Review* 32 (Fall 1958): 33, and for quotes from *Loving v. Virginia,* see George Schuhmann, "Miscegenation: An Example of Judicial Recidivism," *Journal of Family Law* 69 (Spring 1968): 77 along with his thought-provoking note on 74 n. 31. In addition, see "Constitutional Law-Domestic Relations - Miscegenation Laws Based Solely Upon Race Are a Denial of the Due Process and Equal Protection Clauses of the 14th Amendment," *New York Law Forum* 13 (Spring 1967): 170-78;

"The Constitutionality of Miscegenation Statutes," *Howard Law Journal* 1 (January 1955): 92-100; Robert J. Sickels, *Race, Marriage, and the Law* (Albuquerque, 1972); Walter Wadlington, "The *Loving* Case: Virginia's Antimiscegenation Statute in Historical Perspective," *Virginia Law Review* 52 (October 1966): 1189-1223; Andrew D. Weinberger, "A Reappraisal of the Constitutionality of Miscegenation Statutes," *Cornell Law Quarterly* 42 (Winter 1957): 208-22. Also, see Derrick A. Bell, Jr., *Race, Racism and American Law* (Boston, 1973), chap. 6.

5

INTERRACIAL SEXUAL RELATIONS - TO WHAT EXTENT?

Of the white women in the national probability sample, 37% agreed with the belief that many more white men than white women have had interracial sexual relations (Belief Statement 3). The truth of the matter is that many more white men than white women *have* been involved in interracial sexual relations, particularly during slavery days. So many more, that there really is no comparison. In fact, the notion of a white man having sex with a black female slave was even broadcast on national television in the miniseries *Roots.*

From the historical perspective, social custom and convention did not accept sexual relations between white women and black men, a double standard that was able to be maintained because of miscegenation laws and the legal precedences established in Virginia and Maryland back in the mid-1600s. Children born of white mothers and black fathers in following the social status of their mothers would be free mulattoes, and with everything to lose and nothing to gain from such freedom of choice, white men outlawed it. On the other hand, as long as formal interracial marriages were kept illegal, all mulatto children were illegitimate and retained the same social status as their (usually black) mothers.

This policy had its most virulent consequences from the late 1700s through the pre-Civil War antebellum period. For those readers who are unfamiliar with this time in American history and particularly the history of the Southern states, it may be somewhat difficult to truly comprehend the vast extent to which interracial sex occurred. Nowhere can the sexual double standard be seen more clearly than during the period of slavery, when tens of thousands and ultimately several hundred thousand mulatto children were born of slave women and white men. Abraham Lincoln said, "In 1850 there were in the free states, 56,649 mulattoes; but for the most part they were not born there — they came from the slave states, ready made up. In the same year the slave states had 348,874 mulattoes all of home production." By 1860 there were about 70,000 mulattoes in the free states and over 500,000 in the slave states.

It is impossible to know the extent to which interracial sexual relations occurred between white men and black women, but what *is* known is that there were frequent comments on the practice. The following first-person eyewitness accounts will serve to make the point:

Josiah Quincy, Jr., a Massachusetts lawyer who traveled in North and South Carolina (1773):

> The enjoyment of a Negro or mulatto woman is spoken of as quite a common thing: no reluctance, delicacy or shame is made about the matter.
>
> [The famous geographer Jedidiah Morse included Quincy's observation verbatim in his own work (1789), but he also added, "A mischief common, in a greater or less degree, in all the Southern states, at which humanity and decency blush, is the criminal intercourse between the whites and blacks." Morse was not the only one to repeat Quincy's observation. Charles William Janson, an English entrepreneur, included both Quincy and Morse verbatim in a book about his own travels in America (1807).]

Meriwether Jones, journalist and friend of Thomas Jefferson (1802):

> In gentlemen's houses everywhere, we know that the virtue of the unfortunate slaves is assailed with impunity....Is it strange therefore, that a servant of Mr. Jefferson's at a house where so many strangers resort, who is daily engaged in the ordinary vocations of the family, like thousands of others, should have a mulatto child?
>
> [Jones was defending Jefferson against the scurrilous attacks of newspaper editor James T. Callender who charged that the president was having interracial sexual relations with one of his

slave women.   The point here is that Jones
*publicly admitted that thousands of female slaves
were having mulatto children,* "in gentlemen's
houses everywhere."]

Lucius Verus Bierce, a Northerner who traveled extensively throughout the South (1822):

> The manners and customs are similar, after
> crossing the Blue ridge, in Virginia and both
> Carolinas....The vices are drunkness, indolence,
> and among all classes of males, an indiscriminate
> connexion with the female Negroes. This evil has
> extended so far that more than one half of the
> slave population are mixed with the whites.
> [Of course, Bierce had no way of knowing the
> true extent of interracial sexual relations in
> Virginia, North Carolina, and South Carolina,
> however, the practice must have been somewhat
> extensive for him to have made the observation
> he did.]

Isaac Candler, an English traveler (1824):

> A white man may be the father of illegitimate
> mulattoes without being considered a bad
> member of society, or even being shunned by
> virtuous women of the first rank. He may even
> rise to the highest station in the land, and be
> eulogised as a patriot; but if he were to marry the
> mother of his children, he would be considered to
> be degraded past remedy. [Candler reflects on
> the fact that all male legislatures permit this
> social state to exist by law, and comments,] Thus
> virtue is punished and vice escapes. Such are the
> inconsistencies into which men run, when they
> legislate in conformity with prejudice, rather
> than right reason.

Frances Anne Kemble, famed English actress who married Pierce Butler, a wealthy plantation owner (1838):

> Mr.----, and many others, speak as if there were a natural repugnance in all whites to any alliance with the black race; and yet it is notorious, that almost every Southern planter has a family more or less numerous of illegitimate colored children. [Kemble observes,] That such connections exist commonly is a sufficient proof that they are not abhorrent to nature; but it seems, indeed, as if marriage (and not concubinage) was the horrible enormity which cannot be tolerated, and against which, moreover, it has been deemed expedient to enact laws. Now it appears very evident that there is no law in the white man's nature which prevents him from making a colored woman the mother of his children, but there *is* a law on his statute books forbidding him to make her his wife.

Reverend Francis Hawley, a church statesman (1839):

> As it relates to amalgamation, I can say, that I have been in respectable families, (so called,) where I could distinguish the family resemblance in the slaves who waited upon the table....It is so common for the female slaves to have white [light-complexioned mulatto] children, that little or nothing is ever said about it. Very few inquiries are made as to who the father is.

Mary Boykin Chesnut, wife of James Chesnut, Jr., U. S. senator from South Carolina, 1859-1861 (March, 1861):

> Like the patriarches of old our men live all in one house with their wives and their concubines, and the mulattoes one sees in every family exactly resemble the white children — and every lady tells you who is the father of all the mulatto children in everybody's household, but those in her own

> she seems to think drop from the clouds, or
> pretends so to think.

When Southern white men had to address the issue of illicit sexual relations with black women, they invariably pointed a finger at the North with its white prostitution. This line of reasoning is well-illustrated in the writings of South Carolinians William Harper and James Henry Hammond who were politicians, and William Gilmore Simms, a professional writer. The point which necessarily went unaddressed by these men and others, however, was the *context* of this prostitution – the white woman in freedom had choice whereas the black woman in slavery did not.

The interracial sex which occurred between white men and black women was widespread from before the Revolutionary War up to the Civil War. The issue reached far into the contemporary literature of the time, and it may be said that many other references and quotations could have been included here.

Legislation and social standards notwithstanding, white women did have sex with black men, but the historical records which are available indicate only *single isolated instances.* The rate of interracial sex for white women was absolutely minuscule compared to the incidence for white men.

In addition to the interracial sex cases leading up to the Maryland law of 1664 (of which there appear to be no historical records), an early example of sex between a white woman and a black man is the 1685 Massachusetts case of Hannah Bonny and Nimrod, the Negro. Both were whipped and Nimrod was to pay child support for one year, or be bound out by the deputy governor for an equivalent sum. Other cases followed. In 1692 a father whose daughter had "too much Familiarity and Commerce with a Certain Negro Man" petitioned a Maryland court to lower his fine of 6,000 pounds of tobacco. In a Chester County, Pennsylvania case circa 1700 involving interracial fornication, the testimony recorded that "the Negro said she enticed him and promised him to marry him. She being examined, confessed the same...the court ordered that she shall receive twenty-one lashes on her bare back...and the court ordered the Negro never more to meddle with any white woman more upon pain of his life." A North Carolina court case of 1727 revealed that Elizabeth Puckett "hath left her husband and hath for Some years cohabited with a Negro Man of Capt. Simon Jefferies." Also in North Carolina, in a diary entry for 1783, Spanish traveler Francisco de Miranda wrote of Revolutionary War General Robert Howe, "While he amuses himself in dissipation elsewhere, his unfortunate family lives here; the wife has the manner of a divorcee, and one lovely daughter, eighteen years old, has just had two sons by one of the Negro slaves."

Two interesting accounts from the daily newspaper the *Maryland Gazette* are also worth noting:

> Whereas *Mary Skinner,* my Wife, has, after all the Love and Tenderness which could possibly be shown by Man to a Woman, polluted my Bed, by taking to her in my Stead, her own Negro Slave, by whom she hath a Child, which hath occasioned so much Disgrace to me and my Family, that I have thought proper to forbid her my Sight any more, and take this Opportunity to forewarn all Persons whatsoever, from having any Dealings with the said *Mary Skinner* upon my Account, for I hereby declare, that I will not answer any Debts she shall contract in my Name. Given under my Hand this 6th Day of *October,* 1769. WALTER SKINNER.

> Whereas Henrietta, the wife of the subscriber, has committed adultery with a mulatto man, and has now a mulatto child; for which most atrocious crime I have put her away, and do forewarn all persons dealing with her on my account, as I will pay no debts contracted from this tenth day of April, 1773. HENRY PRATT, of Talbot county.

State archives contain divorce petitions filed by white men against their wives for having sex with black men, particularly in the South where plantation and farm women decided to cross the color line themselves. A divorce petition dated December 6, 1815 refers to the candid remarks of a Virginia woman who declared "that she had not been the first nor would she be the last guilty of such conduct, and that she saw no more harm in a white woman's having been the mother of a black [mulatto] child than in a white man's having one, though the latter was more frequent."

In 1853 J. Benwell, an Englishman who traveled in America, acknowledged the great extent to which Southern white men engaged in interracial sex but pointed out that some white women were also involved. He observed, "Nor, from what I gleaned, are the ladies themselves immaculate, as may be inferred from the occasional quadroon aspect of their progeny." Another point of view was that of Thomas L. Nichols, a widely traveled American doctor, who wrote, "The mulattoes in America are the children of black mothers – not otherwise in one case in ten thousand. I never heard of an instance in the South, and of only one or two in the North." Interracial sex involving white women was considered unusual, a fact illustrated by Colonel John Eaton, Jr., General Superintendent of Freedmen, who made special note of six cases in his 1864 Civil War report describing civilian conditions in the Mississippi Valley.

The white women who did have sex with black men dared to challenge the "sanctity of white womanhood" by defying the double standard. The extent to which this sanctity existed is illustrated by judicial cases in which *a mere accusation* of a white woman being sexually involved with a black man was taken to court as an act of slander. Two such cases, for example, occurred in North Carolina in 1818 and Georgia in 1858. To risk slander by even speaking of a white woman in terms of interracial sex exemplifies the judgmental values of a society in which the reins on white women were held tightly by the same white men who had absolute sexual domination over black women. Such sexual domination by white men was acceptable in some quarters and frowned upon in others, but a white woman having sex with a black man was not acceptable and such women were marked with a social stigma. From the historical perspective, all told there were numerous white women who had interracial sexual relations despite the double standard, but their number never approached the multitudes of white men who were likewise involved.

Chapter 5.   INTERRACIAL SEXUAL RELATIONS - TO WHAT EXTENT?

The Collected Works of Abraham Lincoln, ed. Roy P. Basler (New Brunswick, N. J., 1953), 2:408. Lincoln's figures include as a slave "state" the District of Columbia which did not emancipate until 1862. Joseph C. G. Kennedy, *Population of the United States in 1860; Compiled from the Original Returns of the Eighth Census* (Washington, 1864), 598-99.

"Journal of Josiah Quincy, Junior, 1773," ed. Mark A. De Wolfe Howe, *Proceedings of the Massachusetts Historical Society* 49 (June 1916): 463-64; Jedidiah Morse, *The American Geography; or A View of the Present Situation of the United States of America* (1789; reprint, N. Y., 1970), 65; Charles William Janson, *The Stranger in America, 1793-1806* (1807; reprint, ed. Carl S. Driver, N. Y., 1971), 390.

The quote from Meriwether Jones may be had in Fawn M. Brodie, "The Great Jefferson Taboo," *American Heritage* 23 (June 1972): 55. For more on the Jefferson controversy, see Brodie, "Jefferson Biographers and the Psychology of Canonization," *Journal of Interdisciplinary History* 2 (Summer 1971): 155-71.

Travels in the Southland, 1822-1823: The Journal of Lucius Verus Bierce, ed. George W. Knepper (Columbus, Ohio, 1966), 77-78, and also 99-100. Regarding the extent of Bierce's travels, see viii.

[Isaac Candler], *A Summary View of America* (London, 1824), 300-1, and also 299.

Frances Anne Kemble, *Journal of a Residence on a Georgian Plantation in 1838-1839* (1863; reprint, ed. John A. Scott, N. Y., 1961), 10-11 (italics in original), and also 61. Kemble used the word "colored" as the physical description of any black or mulatto. It was commonly used that way in her day. For a view on antipathy similar to that of Kemble's, see Frederick Law Olmsted, *The Cotton Kingdom: A Traveller's Observations on Cotton and Slavery in the American Slave States* (1861; reprint, ed. Arthur M. Schlesinger, N. Y., 1953), 32.

"Narrative and Testimony of Rev. Francis Hawley," in [Theodore D. Weld], *American Slavery as It Is: Testimony of a Thousand Witnesses* (1839; reprint, N. Y., 1968), 97. For other accounts, see 11, 16, 51, 107. A page in this book entitled ADVERTISEMENT TO

THE READER (unnumbered, directly succeeding title page) contains the following:

> A majority of the facts and testimony contained in this work rests upon the authority of SLAVEHOLDERS....Their testimony is taken, mainly, from recent newspapers, published in the slave states. Most of those papers will be deposited at the office of the American Anti-Slavery Society, 143 Nassau Street, New York City. Those who think the atrocities, which they describe, incredible, are invited to call and read for themselves.

Also, see Gilbert Hobbs Barnes, *The Antislavery Impulse, 1830-1844* (N. Y., 1933), 139, 263 n. 20. A review of *American Slavery as It Is* may be had in Dwight Lowell Dumond, *Antislavery: The Crusade for Freedom in America* (Ann Arbor, 1961), chap. 30. Elsewhere Dumond observed, "Hundreds of thousands of copies of the pamphlet were distributed, and its influence was incalculable. There was no effective reply to it, nor could there have been." *Antislavery Origins of the Civil War in the United States* (Ann Arbor, 1959), 42. Regarding the apparent misprint in Professor Thomas R. Dew's pamphlet which was corrected on p. 182 of *American Slavery as It Is,* see Frederic Bancroft, *Slave-Trading in the Old South* (1931; reprint, N. Y., 1959), 72 n. 16.

Mary Chesnut's Civil War, ed. C. Vann Woodward (New Haven, 1981), 29, and also 168-69. These often cited accounts are particularly noteworthy because they were made by a member of the Southern aristocracy.

For the writings of Harper, Hammond, and Simms, see *The Pro-Slavery Argument; as Maintained by the Most Distinguished Writers of the Southern States* (1852; reprint, N. Y., 1968), 40-46, 117-21, 228-30. In 1823 the comments of one antislavery Southerner foreshadowed the Civil War to come. Regarding interracial sexual relations and emancipation, he stated,

> The advocates for African slavery are, no doubt, aware...that the chastity of the coloured females would be less liable to violation, and access to their embraces more difficult to be obtained than

> what they now are...it cannot be wondered at,
> that they persecute the advocates for the universal
> rights of man with such bitterness, for thus
> endeavouring to abridge them in their dearest
> enjoyments....Some of them have publicly
> menaced a dissolution of the Union.

"Philo Humanitas," (letter to the editor), *Genius of Universal Emancipation,* ed. and pub. Benjamin Lundy (Greeneville, Tenn.), 3 (Ninth Month 1823): 43.

Other historical accounts of interracial sex include E. S. Abdy, *Journal of a Residence and Tour in the United States of North America, from April, 1833, to October, 1834* (1835; reprint, N. Y., 1969), 1:306-7, 346-53, 3:126-27; *The Abrogation of the Seventh Commandment, by the American Churches* (N. Y., 1835); Thomas Anburey, *Travels Through the Interior Parts of America* (1789; reprint, N. Y., 1969), 2:372, 385; George Bourne, *Slavery Illustrated in Its Effects Upon Woman and Domestic Society* (Boston, 1837), 23, 90, 96; J. S. Buckingham, *The Slave States of America* (London, 1842), 1:240-41; L. Maria Child, *The Patriarchal Institution, as Described by Members of Its Own Family* (N. Y., 1860), 28-29; Colonel John Eaton, Jr., *Report of the General Superintendent of Freedmen, Department of the Tennessee and State of Arkansas, for 1864* (Memphis, 1865), 93-94; Rev. Charles Elliott, *Sinfulness of American Slavery* (1850; reprint, N. Y., 1968), 1:149-55 and 2:59-66; Rebecca Latimer Felton, *Country Life in Georgia in the Days of My Youth* (Atlanta, 1919), 79; *First Annual Report of the American Anti-Slavery Society* (N. Y., 1834), 27-28; E. Franklin Frazier, *The Negro Family in the United States* (N. Y., 1951), chap. 4; A. E. Grimké, *Letters to Catherine E. Beecher, in Reply to an Essay on Slavery and Abolitionism* (Boston, 1838), 10; Sylvia Hoffert, "This 'One Great Evil'," *American History Illustrated* 12 (May 1977): 37-41; Isaac Holmes, *An Account of the United States of America* (London, 1823), 334; John Dixon Long, *Pictures of Slavery in Church and State* (Phila., 1857), 262-63; Baptist Wriothesley Noel, *Freedom and Slavery in the United States of America* (1863; reprint, Westport, 1970), 82-91; Olmsted, *Cotton Kingdom,* 228-29, 239-40, 472-73 n. 7, 475 n. 1; Alexis de Tocqueville, *Democracy in America* (1838; reprint, ed. Phillips Bradley, N. Y., 1945), 1:374.

Helen Tunnicliff Catterall, ed., *Judicial Cases Concerning*

American Slavery and the Negro (1926; reprint, N. Y., 1968), 4:478, 28; Edward R. Turner, *The Negro in Pennsylvania* (Washington, 1911), 30 n. 37. For more on early interracial cases involving white women, see Robert C. Twombly and Robert H. Moore, "Black Puritan: The Negro in Seventeenth-Century Massachusetts," *William and Mary Quarterly* 24 (April 1967): 230-31. Catterall, *Judicial Cases* 2:12; *The New Democracy in America: Travels of Francisco de Miranda in the United States, 1783-84,* trans. Judson P. Wood, ed. John S. Ezell (Norman, Okla., 1963), 14.

Maryland Gazette, 12 Oct. 1769, p. 2 (italics in original), and 22 April 1773, p. 2.

Regarding divorce cases, see James Hugo Johnston, *Race Relations in Virginia and Miscegenation in the South, 1776-1860* (Amherst, Mass., 1970), chap. 10, quote on 267-68, and Catterall, *Judicial Cases,* indexes for "Divorce" and related entries. Also, see Herbert G. Gutman, *The Black Family in Slavery and Freedom, 1750-1925* (N. Y., Vintage Books, 1976), 614-16 n. 13, and William Lloyd Imes, "The Legal Status of Free Negroes and Slaves in Tennessee," *Journal of Negro History* 4 (July 1919): 272.

J. Benwell, *An Englishman's Travels in America: His Observations of Life and Manners in the Free and Slave States* (London, [1853]), 205. Thomas L. Nichols, *Forty Years of American Life* (1864; reprint, N. Y., 1969), 2:235. In the same paragraph Nichols draws a comparison between England and America:

> In England Negroes are soon married to decent seeming white women. Negroes may be met escorting fashionably dressed ladies. White women walk in the streets with their mulatto children. There is scarcely a town in America where such things could be done without exciting violent manifestations of public indignation.

Eaton, *Report of the General Superintendent,* 93.

For examples of slander cases, see Catterall, *Judicial Cases* 2:35 and 3:67. Historian Guion G. Johnson states that in North Carolina, some husbands seeking divorce from their wives falsely accused them of interracial involvements. *Ante-Bellum North Carolina* (Chapel Hill, 1937), 588-89.

6

IS THERE REALLY A SEXUAL DIFFERENCE?

In the national probability sample of white women, only 17% were in agreement with the belief that the sexuality of an average white man is somehow different than that of an average Afro-American man (Belief Statement 4), yet 41% agreed with the belief that many white men view their own sexuality as being somehow different (Belief Statement 5). That is to say, there was a sharp contrast in the survey findings between what white women believe for themselves and what they perceive the beliefs of white men to be. In light of the complex nature of the issues involved, there is no way of determining what the women had in mind when they responded to the two statements about male sexuality.

Sexuality is not a constant. On the contrary, it involves many different mental and physical components which are influenced by many vicissitudes and subjectivities. For example, men may feel more sexual sometimes as opposed to other times, and given a particularly stimulating context of atmosphere, place, or partner, sexual performance may exceed individual norms. On the other hand, given different contexts, performance may be less or far less than average. (This would account for the normal occasional impotency experienced by many men.) The subjective components of male sexuality such as desire, performance motivation, coital prolongation, and orgasmic capacity all differ from individual to individual as well as from circumstance to circumstance. There is one component of male sexuality, however, that *can* be addressed objectively, and that is the male sexual organ.

Of all the aspects in a discussion about male sexuality, particularly black male sexuality, it may be said that none is as controversial as penis size. So much myth, imagination, and misinformation abound that the truth of the matter is not commonly known. What *is* the truth? Although available information is very limited, the data of Alfred C. Kinsey and other professionals appear to draw the same

TABLE 70. MEASURED LENGTH OF ERECT PENIS

LENGTH TO NEAREST QUARTER INCH	MALE		
	White		Black
	College	Non College	College
	%	%	%
-2.75	0	0	0
3.00	--	0	0
3.25	0	0	0
3.50	0	0	0
3.75	0.2	0.7	0
4.00	0.3	1.4	0
4.25	0.2	0	0
4.50	1.7	1.4	0
4.75	0.8	1.4	0
5.00	4.2	7.0	3.4
5.25	4.4	4.2	1.7
5.50	10.7	8.4	5.1
5.75	8.0	2.8	5.1
6.00	23.9	23.8	25.4
6.25	8.8	10.5	10.2
6.50	14.3	15.4	16.9
6.75	5.7	5.6	6.8
7.00	9.5	9.8	11.9
7.25	1.8	1.4	5.1
7.50	2.9	2.8	1.7
7.75	1.0	2.1	1.7
8.00	1.0	0.7	1.7
8.25	0.3	0	1.7
8.50	0.3	0	0
8.75	0.1	0	0
9.00	0.1	0	1.7
9.25	0	0.7	0
9.50	0	0	0
9.75	0	0	0
10.00+	0	0	0
Known N	2376	143	59
Unknown N	2318	623	118
Inapplicable N	0	0	0
Card and column	7/42-43		

STANDARD QUESTION: None. Respondents were given cards to fill out and return in preaddressed stamped envelopes, and were instructed to measure on the top surface from belly to tip of penis.

TABLE 71. MEASURED LENGTH OF FLACCID PENIS

LENGTH TO NEAREST QUARTER INCH	MALE		
	White		Black
	College	Non College	College
	%	%	%
1.50	0.1	1.4	0
1.75	0.1	0	0
2.00	0.9	2.1	0
2.25	0.5	1.4	1.7
2.50	2.7	2.8	1.7
2.75	1.6	2.1	0
3.00	10.0	12.0	0
3.25	5.3	4.2	1.7
3.50	17.3	18.3	6.8
3.75	8.4	6.3	8.5
4.00	21.7	21.1	18.6
4.25	6.2	6.3	6.8
4.50	13.8	10.6	22.0
4.75	3.7	1.4	10.2
5.00	4.4	4.9	11.9
5.25	1.0	0	5.1
5.50	1.5	3.5	5.1
5.75	0.3	0.7	0
6.00	0.3	0.7	0
6.25	--	0	0
6.50	0.1	0	0
6.75	0	0	0
7.00	0	0	0
7.25	0	0	0
7.50	0	0	0
7.75	0	0	0
8.00+	--	0	0
Known N	2379	142	59
Unknown N	2315	624	118
Inapplicable N	0	0	0
Card and column	7/40-41		

STANDARD QUESTION: None. Respondents were given cards to fill out and return in preaddressed stamped envelopes.

NOTE: The Noncollege Black group as well as other groups were not included in the basic sample because of problems with data. Paul H.Gebhard and Alan B. Johnson explain, "Defects of sample also forced us to omit Blacks of less-than-college education." *(THE KINSEY DATA: Marginal Tabulations of the 1938-1963 Interviews Conducted by the Institute for Sex Research* [Phila.: W. B. Saunders, 1979], 4.)

conclusion. Generally speaking, the penis of an average black man is comparable in size to that of an average white man in its erect state; however, in its *flaccid* (unerect) state, it can be slightly larger in some instances. The word *larger,* it is to be understood, refers only to small fractions of an inch. These small fractional differences have been tabulated in TABLE 71 from the Kinsey Institute for Sex Research (now the Kinsey Institute for Research in Sex, Gender, and Reproduction).

In 1979 this internationally famous institute published several hundred statistical tables regarding various aspects of sexuality with separate data for whites and blacks. Two of these tables deal with erect and flaccid penis lengths, and the data speak for themselves. In TABLE 70 the most significant statistics are those which show that 6 inches was the most frequent erect penis measurement *for both white men and black men.* Other figures for both whites and blacks are virtually within a few percentage points of each other. In TABLE 71 the flaccid penis measurements show a much greater disparity, with more black men having flaccid lengths between 4½ inches and 5¼ inches. Worth noting is the fact that white men had the longest lengths in both the erect and flaccid measurement tables.

In speaking of the Kinsey data, it is important to point out that the men involved measured themselves. How valid were these self-measurements? Dr. Robert Latou Dickinson in his classic work *Atlas of Human Sex Anatomy* reviewed the existing literature on penis size and found nine professionals who had measurements for the flaccid and erect penis (among white men, who comprised virtually all of the data). Dickinson computed these statistics and concluded, "Averages made up from the statements of the nine authors who give any data show the flaccid penis 10 cm. in length and 3 cm. in diameter, and 8.5 cm. in circumference (4″ x 1-1/8″ x 3-3/8″); and the erect penis 15.5 cm. long, 4 cm. broad and 11 cm. around (6″ x 1-5/8″ x 4-3/8″)." When one compares these figures with those in TABLES 70 and 71, it is plain to see that Dickinson's averages and Kinsey's most frequently reported measurements are the same – 6 inches erect and 4 inches flaccid. No doubt there were errors in self-measurement in the Kinsey data, however, overall at least for white men, these data appear to be valid as evidenced by the comparison with Dickinson's averages.

Other professional literature has addressed the male sexual organ, and although erection has been reported accurately, flaccid size has been subjected to unfortunate generalizations. Sociologist Robert Staples has published much on the subject of black sexuality and observes, "It has been noted that, although the penis of the Negro male is larger than that of his white counterpart when flaccid, there is no significant difference between the penis size of the two groups when in an erect form." Sexologist James L. McCary has said, "It is believed by some that because body configurations of black and white males are somewhat different, the flaccid penis of the Negro is accordingly slightly larger than that of the white man. Scientific investigations that involved careful measurement of the sex organs have shown that, indeed, the flaccid penis of the average black male is slightly longer than that of the white man. However, there appears to be little or no relationship between the size of any penis when flaccid and its size when erect." In speaking of the inconsistency of size, Dr. John F. Oliven states, "Nor is a penis which is small in the resting stage also necessarily small when erect, nor a large pendulous organ necessarily transformed into a large-sized erection. Racial differences in erective size do not exist to any significant degree in the U. S. population. The penis of many black men appears relatively large in the flaccid state, even without the often characteristic long prepuce, but there seems to be a proportionately lesser increase in erective length."

Such observations are not limited to the twentieth century. In 1865 William Acton, a famous sexologist of his day, wrote of the flaccid penis, "In the Negro it is proverbially large, but, as in the case in whites also who have the same peculiarity, does not proportionately increase in size on erection taking place." In later editions, Acton added, "A small penis, it should also be remembered, when in a state of erection often exceeds in size one which is larger while in a quiescent state."

A great many men do not understand that regardless of race, smaller and larger flaccid sexual organs erect somewhat differently. A smaller one may double in length in its erect state, whereas a larger one will increase to a much lesser extent. Masters and Johnson, world-renowned pioneers in the field of sex research, refer to the flaccid penis and observe, "It has been presumed that full erection of the larger penis provides a significantly greater penile size increase than does erection of the smaller penis." They dispel this belief by stating, "The difference in average erective size increase between the smaller flaccid penis and the larger flaccid penis is not significant."

Psychological implications regarding penis size are clear. Not knowing that smaller and larger flaccid organs erect to different proportions has led to a profound misunderstanding on the part of many white men. Men go to health clubs and to the gymnasium to participate in sports and other recreational activities and are naked when changing in and out of street clothes and when showering. In what might well be termed the "Locker Room Reaction," a white man who does not know about the relationship between flaccid size and erection physiology may see a longer flaccid penis of a black man and *imagine* it to be extraordinarily large in erection. For a white man to react this way is entirely understandable because of the absence of knowledge to the contrary. Such white men would no doubt be surprised to learn that in an erect state, many black and white penises are really comparable in size.

Further adding to the white man's misconception in the locker room is the common belief that size somehow influences virility, and this is also absolutely untrue. As Masters and Johnson have said, "Another widely accepted 'phallic fallacy' is the concept that the larger the penis the more effective the male as a partner in coital connection." Even William Acton back in 1865 observed, "*Size, I may here again remark, is no sign of vigor.*" If a man with a larger penis is commonly imagined to be more virile, and a black man with a larger (flaccid) penis is observed in the locker room, many white men making such an observation could readily feel their own virility threatened. Despite available factual information, it is easy to see how associating a larger flaccid penis with a superior virility might lead some white men to view their own sexuality as different than that of Afro-American men and perhaps feel some degree of sexual anxiety as a consequence. Moreover, it is to be remembered that while a penis attains its own particular size each time it is in a state of complete erection, a vagina is a *potential* space, capable of expanding to accommodate a wide range of sizes, i.e., a tampon, baby, or penis.

———————

The same sexual misunderstandings which twentieth-century white men might experience in the locker room may well have been experienced by eighteenth and nineteenth-century white men as well, especially on Southern plantations whenever naked slaves were seen. Although few historians discuss the subject, the numerous first-person eyewitness accounts which exist indicate that nakedness among slaves throughout the South was not uncommon, particularly during the summer months, and also during the Revolutionary War period when war shortages made clothing exceedingly difficult to obtain. Most significant, however, is the fact that throughout the entire antebellum period up to the Civil War it was common practice to give slaves a certain clothing allotment each year, and some masters did not provide additional replacements if these clothes wore out. Among the many examples of slave nakedness in general that could be cited, those which follow will serve to make the point. Joseph Ide, postmaster of Sheffield, Vermont, traveled in the South during 1838 and 1839 and reported seeing "from forty to sixty, male and female, at work in a field, many of both sexes with their bodies entirely naked." In 1850 the Rev. Charles Elliott wrote of "the fieldhands and the children, both male and female, whose nakedness is shamelessly exposed, at the expense both of modesty and decorum."

Some travelers throughout the South during the latter part of the eighteenth century made particular mention of slave nudity and white women being indifferent to it:

Ferdinand M. Bayard, a Frenchman who came to America during the time of the French Revolution (1791):

> In all the states where slavery is permitted, the women tolerate nakedness which would disconcert the least modest European woman. They declare that in the southern part of Virginia, in the two Carolinas, in Georgia and even in Charlestown, young Negroes, absolutely naked, appear before their mistresses, serve them at the table, without their suspecting that that is indecent. I have seen young girls, standing behind a palingfence, staring at the naked form of a Negro man who was being whipped.

Johann David Schoepf, German physician and naturalist (1783):

> Our European ladies would be horrified to see about them Negroes and Negresses in a costume which starts no blush here.

George Grieve, English businessman and traveler (1782?):

> It was a singular sight for an European to behold the situation of the Negroes in the southern provinces during the war, when clothing was extremely scarce. I have frequently seen in Virginia, on visits to gentlemen's houses, young

> Negroes and Negresses running about or basking in the courtyard naked as they came into the world, with well characterized marks of perfect puberty; and young Negroes from sixteen to twenty years old, with not an article of clothing, but a loose shirt, descending half way down their thighs, waiting at table where were ladies, without any apparent embarrassment on one side, or the slightest attempt at concealment on the other.

Ebenezer Hazard, a Philadelphian traveling through Virginia (1777):

> The Virginians, even in the City, do not pay proper Attention to Decency in the Appearance of their Negroes; I have seen Boys of 10 & 12 Years of Age going through the Streets quite naked, & others with only Part of a Shirt hanging Part of the Way down their Backs. This is so common a sight that even the Ladies do not appear to be shocked at it.

Certainly, most slaves were clothed most of the time, yet judging from historical accounts, slave nudity must have been considered uneventful when it did occur. Nevertheless, naked slaves must have had profound effects on many whites, not the least of which being sexual titillation. The large extent to which white men had sexual relations with black women illustrates this point. On the other hand, white women titillated or not generally succumbed to the social standards of the day and responded with indifference.

Besides the contemporary written accounts of the time, there is one additional case to be addressed concerning slave nudity and that is the physical inspection of slaves at the slave auctions. Prior to an auction, as a matter of common practice, slaves were inspected for diseases such as tetanus, worm infections, and yaws. Such inspections were conducted by those involved with the procurement, sale, and distribution of slaves. Several contemporary first-person eyewitness accounts describe the activities:

William Chambers, prominent British publisher (1854):

The next lot brought forward was one of the men....The man placidly rose, and having been placed behind the screen, was ordered to take off his clothes, which he did without a word or look of remonstrance. About a dozen gentlemen crowded to the spot while the poor fellow was stripping himself, and as soon as he stood on the floor, bare from top to toe, a most rigorous scrutiny of his person was instituted. The clear black skin, back and front, was viewed all over for sores from disease; and *there was no part of his body left unexamined.* [In another reference, Chambers refers to] the usual scrutiny behind a screen.

Charles Richard Weld, barrister and librarian of the Royal Society (1855):

There were four men, and two girls. The former were immediately led behind the screen, *stripped stark naked, and examined with great minuteness.*...The women were more tenderly dealt with. Personal examination was confined to the hands, arms, legs, bust, and teeth....It is unnecessary to carry the reader to the other slave marts.

James Redpath, journalist and author (1859):

The slave was dressed in his pantaloons, shirt and vest. His vest was removed and his breast and neck exposed. His shoes and stockings were next taken off and his legs beneath the knees examined. His other garment was then loosened, and *his naked body, from the upper part of the abdomen to the knees,* was shamelessly exhibited to the view of the spectators.

The inspection of slaves at the slave auctions had as a consequence an irony of perspective. When one looks at an object up close, the object appears much larger than if viewed at some distance away, and looking at a naked black man out in a field was certainly a very different perception than conducting an examination up close at a slave auction. This latter viewpoint had the effect of making the flaccid sexual organ look bigger than its actual size.

One might argue that only a small portion of whites owned slaves and therefore the sight of slave nakedness would be confined to this limited population. While it is true that only about one-fourth of the white population in the slave states held slaves, many other people came into visual contact with them. In addition to those who conducted commerce in slaves, travelers on horseback, in a carriage, or on a train could see slaves working in the fields as they passed by, visitors to plantations also saw them, and slave auctions were open to the public. At any rate, whether white men perceived slave nakedness from the perspective of the field, the city street (as in the account of Ebenezer Hazard), the plantation house, or the auction, one cannot help but think that some of them might well have experienced the same feelings as those had by twentieth-century white men in the "Locker Room Reaction" described earlier in this chapter.

If black men were thought to have a greater virility, the idea certainly found support in the *artificial* sexual behavior which many black women must have displayed when necessary as a response to the sexual advances made toward them by white men. It must be understood that if a slave woman did not voluntarily submit to the will of her white master, she risked physical abuse and would have to yield anyway. On the other hand, becoming a white man's favorite brought with it the possibilities of a better life style as well as much less risk of being sold off into the unknown. Black female slaves *living in a daily condition of utter survival* had everything to gain by acting sexually responsive. How were these black women perceived by the white men with whom they interacted? *Artificial* sexual behavior was misconstrued to be *natural* sexual behavior. This idea seems quite plausible when considered in terms of the psychological ego defense mechanism known as *projection,* the externalizing of one's own undesirable impulses by attributing them to others. Here, a white master or other white man might experience anxiety and guilt about having sexual feelings toward a black woman, but in terms of projection, these sexual feelings would be perceived as belonging to the black woman who was expressing them toward him. Projection avoided an inner conflict of ambivalent sexual feelings toward the black woman because unconscious repressed impulses upon reaching the conscious level were disowned. Simply stated, it was the idea of "I don't want her, she wants me." In reality of course, if white masters and other white men truly did not desire black women, the scene just described could never have been played. This desire was no doubt fueled by the puritanical sexuality imposed on white women in those days. Ironically, under slavery the sexual identities of both black women and white women were incomplete. As historian Minrose C. Gwin has commented, "Female narrators of the slave narratives reveal their yearning for the chaste respectability of their white sisters, while the diaries and memoirs of the white women show their intense jealousy of the stereotypical sexuality of the slave woman. Each is only one half of a self."

Be that as it may, the following generalization posed the problem: if black women possessed (were perceived to possess) a sexuality that was naturally responsive and "superior" to that of white women, then black men might also be of this nature and could be as equally enjoyed by white women. In the absence of knowledge, *imagination* entered the picture. The thought that the black man could be as sexually "superior" as the black woman was perceived to be, became the thought that he was so, and his flaccid penis size was "proof." As has been shown, beginning in the mid-1600s with *partus sequitur ventrem* on the one hand and "lascivious and lustful desires" on the other (see Chapter 4), for 300 years the colonial and state laws prohibiting interracial sexual relations were sponsored, legislated, and supported by white men. To what extent can this legislation and its long legacy be interpreted as a response to white men believing that their sexual competence was threatened?

One last perspective is worth looking at, and that is the difference between blacks and American Indians in the thinking of a colonial white man. Georges Louis Leclerc de Buffon, the famous French naturalist and member of the French Academy, claimed that "the savage is feeble and small in his organs of generation." Buffon's idea of small Indian genitalia as well as other accusations against the Indian were included and refuted by Thomas Jefferson in his widely read book, *Notes on the State of Virginia* (1787). Jefferson's book also included commentaries by Charles Thomson who was secretary of Congress and a personal friend. Thomson wrote, "But he [Buffon] says their organs of generation are smaller and weaker than those of Europeans. Is this a fact? I believe not; at least it is an observation I never heard before." Unlike the black man, the flaccid penis of the Indian was not thought of as being larger and therefore *posed no threat* to the sexual competence of a colonial white man. In fact, most laws prohibiting interracial sexual relations did not even include the Indian.

When viewed in terms of America's past, it has been seen that the fear of penis inadequacy, the psychology of the "Locker Room Reaction," and sexual misunderstandings have had a long history. All that can be said for the eighteenth and nineteenth-century American white man can be said for the twentieth-century American white man as well. With ignorance feeding on myth, it is easy to see how these ideas began and continue to be perpetuated.

Chapter 6. IS THERE REALLY A SEXUAL DIFFERENCE?

Paul H. Gebhard and Alan B. Johnson, *THE KINSEY DATA: Marginal Tabulations of the 1938-1963 Interviews Conducted by the Institute for Sex Research* (Phila., 1979), 117, 118. Regarding other penis data, TABLES 72 and 73 give the percentages for flaccid circumference and erect circumference, and these figures are comparable as well. See 119, 120. Alan P. Bell has made generalizations about data from the Kinsey sample. "Black Sexuality: Fact and Fancy" (Paper presented to *Focus: Black America* series, Indiana University, Bloomington, Indiana, 14 October 1968), 11. Robert Latou Dickinson, *Atlas of Human Sex Anatomy*, 2d ed. (Baltimore, 1949), 74. The nine professionals cited were the following: Krause (1879), Waldeyer (1889), Loeb (1899), Debbet (1901), Piersol (1907), White and Martin (1911), Testut and Jacob (1914), Keyes (1917), Testut and Latarjet (1931).

Robert Staples, "Negro-White Sex: Fact and Fiction," in *The Black Family: Essays and Studies,* ed. R. Staples (Belmont, Cal., 1971), 290; James Leslie McCary, *Sexual Myths and Fallacies* (1971; N.Y., Schocken Paperback, 1973), 43; John F. Oliven, *Clinical Sexuality: A Manual for the Physician and the Professions,* 3d ed. (Phila., 1974), 168; William Acton, *The Functions and Disorders of the Reproductive Organs in Childhood, Youth, Adult Age, and Advanced Life,* from the latest London ed., (Phila., 1865), 157, and for example, the 1883 edition, 75. Acton may have had an unusually good understanding of erection physiology in the male, but his knowledge of female sexuality left much to be desired: "The majority of women (happily for them) are not very much troubled with sexual feelings of any kind. What men are habitually, women are only exceptionally." *Functions and Disorders,* 133.

William H. Masters and Virginia E. Johnson, *Human Sexual Response* (Boston, 1966), 191, 192. They go on to state that "the smaller penis in the flaccid state usually remains somewhat smaller in an erect state," however, measurements were conducted to the nearest 0.5 cm, and they did conclude that the difference at issue was "not significant." See 192, 193.

Masters and Johnson, *Human Sexual Response,* 191; Acton, *Functions and Disorders,* 157 (italics in original). Many experts have addressed the subject of penis anxiety. Among others, see Alex

Comfort, "Anxiety Over Penile Size," *Medical Aspects of Human Sexuality* 14 (September 1980): 121+; Igor Grant, "Quiz," *Medical Aspects of Human Sexuality* 9 (May 1975): 111; Emil Steinberger, "Quiz: Patients' Most Common Questions about Sexual Anatomy," *Medical Aspects of Human Sexuality* 15 (August 1981): 110-11; Max Sugar, "Teenager's Concern about Penis Size," *Medical Aspects of Human Sexuality* 16 (September 1982): 97-98; Povl W. Toussieng, "Men's Fear of Having Too Small a Penis," *Medical Aspects of Human Sexuality* 11 (May 1977): 62+.

"Testimony of Joseph Ide, Esq.," in [Theodore D. Weld], *American Slavery as It Is: Testimony of a Thousand Witnesses* (1839; reprint, N. Y., 1968), 101; Charles Elliott, *Sinfulness of American Slavery* (1850; reprint, N. Y., 1968), 1:210.   Other eyewitness accounts attesting to slave nakedness include Thomas Anburey, *Travels Through the Interior Parts of America* (1789; reprint, N. Y., 1969), 2:333; George Bourne, *Slavery Illustrated in Its Effects Upon Woman and Domestic Society* (Boston, 1837), 98; J[acques] P[ierre] Brissot de Warville, *New Travels in the United States of America, 1788,* trans. Mara S. Vamos, ed. Durand Echeverria (Cambridge, Mass., 1964), 231, 233, 339; John Davis, *Travels of Four Years and a Half in the United States of America During 1798, 1799, 1800, 1801, and 1802,* ed. A. J. Morrison (N. Y., 1909), 422; "The Journal of Lieutenant William Feltman, May 26, 1781 to April 25, 1782," *Collections of the Historical Society of Pennsylvania* (Phila., 1853), 1:304-5; Charles William Janson, *The Stranger in America, 1793-1806* (1807; reprint, ed. Carl S. Driver, N. Y., 1971), 381-82; "Diary of the Hon. Jonathan Mason, communicated by George E. Ellis," *Proceedings of the Massachusetts Historical Society,* 2d ser., 2 (1885-86), 22; Johann David Schoepf, *Travels in the Confederation [1783-1784],* trans. and ed. Alfred J. Morrison (Phila., 1911), 2:147; [Weld], *American Slavery,* 19, 40.

Ferdinand M. Bayard, *Travels of a Frenchman in Maryland and Virginia with a Description of Philadelphia and Baltimore in 1791,* trans. and ed. Ben C. McCary (Ann Arbor, 1950), 20; Schoepf, *Travels* 1:357; Marquis de Chastellux, *Travels in North America in the Years 1780, 1781 and 1782,* ed. and trans. Howard C. Rice, Jr. (Chapel Hill, 1963), 2:585 n. 19.   George Grieve was the contemporary translator of Chastellux's book and liberally added many of his own observations about America in the form of footnotes which he included throughout the text. Also, see James O'Kelly, *Essay on Negro-Slavery* (Phila., 1789), 26, and Robert Sutcliff, *Travels in Some Parts of North America in the Years 1804, 1805, & 1806* (London, 1811), 98. "The Journal of Ebenezer Hazard in Virginia, 1777," ed. Fred Shelley, *Virginia Magazine of History and Biography* 62 (October 1954): 410. Other references which describe adult Negroes wearing only a shirt include *Journal of a Tour to North Carolina by William Attmore, 1787,* ed. Lida Tunstall Rodman (Chapel Hill, 1922), 25; *The Journal of Claude Blanchard... 1780-1783,* trans. William Duane, ed. Thomas Balch (Albany, 1876), 163; *Maryland Gazette,* 16 Sept. 1790, p. 2. Also, see John Brickell, *The Natural History of North-Carolina* (1737; reprint, Raleigh, 1911), 276; James O. Breeden, ed., *Advice Among Masters: The Ideal in Slave Management in the Old South* (Westport, 1980), 287; Martha H. Brown, "Clothing," in *Dictionary of Afro-American Slavery,* ed. Randall M. Miller and John David Smith (N. Y., 1988), 118.

   William Chambers, *Things as They Are in America* (1854; reprint, N. Y., 1968), 281, 283 (italics added). Frederick Law Olmsted chose to include this account in his own work, *The Cotton Kingdom: A Traveller's Observations on Cotton and Slavery in the American Slave States* (1861; reprint, ed. Arthur M. Schlesinger, N. Y., 1953), Appendix B; Charles Richard Weld, *A Vacation Tour in the United States and Canada* (London, 1855), 299-300 (italics added), 304; James Redpath, *The Roving Editor: or, Talks with Slaves in the Southern States* (1859; reprint, N. Y., 1968), 9-10 (italics added), and 184, 247. Also, see *The Anti-Slavery Bugle,* 10 April 1852, p. 1; [George Washington Carleton], *The Suppressed Book about Slavery! Prepared for Publication in 1857, - Never Published Until the Present Time* (1864; reprint, N. Y., 1968), 142-43; Gerald G. Eggert, "A Pennsylvanian Visits the Richmond Slave Market," *Pennsylvania Magazine of History and Biography* 109 (October 1985): 572, 575. The purchase of slaves occasionally involved women buyers. At a slave auction in Dutch Guiana in 1808, Captain Richard Drake observed, "Some of the Dutch maids are good looking, in their short green jackets and scarlet petticoats; they moved about, inspecting the naked Africans, as if it was a common thing." *Revelations of a Slave Smuggler: Being the Autobiography of Capt. Rich'd Drake, an African Trader for Fifty*

Years — from 1807 to 1857 (1860; reprint, Northbrook, Ill., 1972), 45.

In regard to the white slaveholding population, according to the census of 1860 there were 384,884 heads of families or agents who were slaveholders. The census states, "It would probably be a safe rule to consider the number of slaveholders to represent the number of families directly interested in the slave population in 1860." Inasmuch as the average family at that time consisted of about five persons, the approximate number of whites involved as slaveholders would be around two million, or about one-fourth of a total white population of over eight million for the slaveholding region. Joseph C. G. Kennedy, *Agriculture of the United States in 1860; Compiled from the Original Returns of the Eighth Census* (Washington, 1864), clxxii, 247 and his *Population of the United States in 1860; Compiled from the Original Returns of the Eighth Census* (Washington, 1864), 598-99; *Statistics of the United States, (Including Mortality, Property, &c.,) in 1860; Compiled from the Original Returns and Being the Final Exhibit of the Eighth Census* (Washington, 1866), 351.

For examples of artificial sexual behavior toward white men, see *Mary Chesnut's Civil War,* ed. C. Vann Woodward (New Haven, 1981), 15, and Davis, *Travels,* 400, 415. An example of the stereotype such behavior produced may be had in George Tucker, *Progress of the United States in Population and Wealth in Fifty Years* (1855; reprint, N. Y., 1964), 98. Minrose C. Gwin, *Black and White Women of the Old South: The Peculiar Sisterhood in American Literature* (Knoxville, Tenn., 1985), 11, also 4-5, 46-48, 79. Harry Elmer Barnes asks, "Was not Southern chivalry a collective compensation for sexual looseness, racial intermixture, and the maltreatment of the Negro?" "Psychology and History: Some Reasons for Predicting Their More Active Cooperation in the Future," *American Journal of Psychology* 30 (October 1919): 374.

For more on the ego defense mechanism of projection as it relates to interracial sexual relations, see Gordon W. Allport, *The Nature of Prejudice* (Boston, 1954), 375-76; George M. Fredrickson, *The Arrogance of Race* (Middletown, Conn., 1988), 191; Lawrence J. Friedman, *The White Savage: Racial Fantasies in the Postbellum South* (Englewood Cliffs, N. J., Spectrum Book, 1970), 10-11; Winthrop D. Jordan, *White Over Black: American Attitudes*

Toward the Negro, 1550-1812 (Chapel Hill, 1968), 151-52; Lillian Smith, *Killers of the Dream* (N. Y., 1949), 116-17; James W. Vander Zanden, *American Minority Relations: The Sociology of Race and Ethnic Groups,* 2d ed. (N. Y., 1966), 175-78. For projection in general, see Allport, *Nature of Prejudice,* chap. 24; John Dollard and Neal E. Miller, *Personality and Psychotherapy: An Analysis in Terms of Learning, Thinking, and Culture* (N. Y., 1950), 181-84; Ludwig Eidelberg, "Projection," in *Encyclopedia of Psychoanalysis* (N. Y., 1968), 331-32; H. P. Laughlin, *The Ego and Its Defenses,* 2d ed. (N. Y., 1979), chap. 15.

This conception of Indian genitalia which Buffon included in his *Histoire Naturelle* series (volume nine, 1761) was picked up and repeated by Cornelius de Pauw in his own work, *Recherches Philosophiques sur les Américains* (1768). *Sketches of the History of Man* (1774) by Henry Home (Lord Kames) also included Buffon's idea that Indians were "feeble in their organs of generation." Antonello Gerbi, *The Dispute of the New World: The History of a Polemic, 1750-1900,* trans. Jeremy Moyle (Pittsburgh, 1973), 6, 178; Henry S. Commager and Elmo Giordanetti, *Was America a Mistake? An Eighteenth-Century Controversy* (N. Y., Harper Torchbooks, 1967), 60, 90-91. Thomas Jefferson, *Notes on the State of Virginia* (1787; reprint, ed. William Peden, N. Y., 1972), 58-64, quote on 200. Regarding Indians and colonial laws banning interracial sexual relations, see Jordan, *White Over Black,* 163.

7

HOW DO WE INHERIT OUR SKIN COLOR?

Of the white women in the national probability sample, 63% agreed with the belief that a white woman and a light-complexioned Afro-American man could have a child with a darker complexion than the man (Belief Statement 6). Inasmuch as it is a *genetic impossibility* for these two people to have such a child, this survey finding shows that skin color inheritance is an often misunderstood phenomenon. In order to understand the process involved here, three different unions will be discussed – white and black, white and mulatto, mulatto and mulatto.

When a white and a black mate, their child will be an intermediate combination of the all light skin color genes of one parent and the all dark skin color genes of the other parent. (Pigment-producing skin color genes may vary in potency which explains the reason several offspring of a white and a black may differ slightly in shade from one another.) This child is a true "mulatto" in the strict definition of the word, although it is important to note that the term is commonly taken to mean a person with *any degree* of white and black admixture. In 1578, in an overstatement typical of the exaggerated literary style of the time, commentator George Best described a genetic impossibility when he wrote that a white and a black had a black child:

> I myself have seen a Negro as black as a coal
> brought into England, who taking a fair English
> woman to wife, begat a son in all respects as
> black as the father was.

In this case the child would be a mulatto and would have to be lighter than its father.

When a white and a mulatto of any degree mate, the situation is different. The light skin color genes from the white parent and the light and dark skin color genes from the mulatto parent can combine in *any* combination. There are *at least* three pairs of genes at work in skin color inheritance so many combinations are possible. *With reference to Belief Statement 6, as long as one parent is white and is contributing light skin color genes, the child will always be lighter in color than the other mulatto parent whether dark or light-complexioned.* On extremely rare occasions interracial couples have produced sets of twins with very different skin colors. Two such cases exist in England – the Smith twins and the Charnock twins. In each instance one child is light-complexioned and the other is dark-complexioned. As extraordinary as this may be for twins, the laws of skin color inheritance still hold because one parent is white in each case and neither of the darker children is any darker than the dark-complexioned parent.

When two mulattoes of any degree mate, each contributes both light *and* dark skin color genes. The child can get all or most of the dark skin color genes from both parents and be darker than either parent; the child can get all or most of the light skin color genes from both parents and be lighter than either parent; the child can get any combination of light and dark skin color genes from both parents and be whatever color that combination dictates. This principle can be illustrated in the pre-Civil War work of historian Kenneth M. Stampp. In examining manuscript census returns for 1860, he found that slave mothers who were listed as "Mulatto" often had children who were listed as "Black." Their dark color is readily explained by laws of genetic skin color inheritance whereby two mulattoes *can* produce a child darker than either parent. The children referred to in the census data had mulatto mothers and either mulatto or black fathers.

As long as a mulatto of any degree continues to mate with white, skin color will necessarily lighten. Marquis de Chastellux, a major-general in the French Army and one of only forty members of the prestigious French Academy, knew this truth over 200 years ago. In 1787 he wrote of white men marrying black women, which "would give rise to a race of mulattoes, which would in turn produce a race of quadroons [theoretically one-fourth black], and so on, until the color would be totally changed." Likewise, in 1823 "Philo Humanitas" (pseudonym used by an antislavery Southerner) expressed the idea that slavery would be abolished because of the great extent to which interracial sexual relations occurred in the South. He concluded that everyone would end up having the same complexion "which will be esteemed white by the inhabitants." Philo invented a new name for this process "which for the want of a more appropriate term, I shall call the *whitening operation.*" Even the proslavery writer William Gilmore Simms called attention to the dynamics of skin color inheritance. In 1838 he wrote, "In the progress of a few generations, that, which might otherwise forever prove a separating wall between the white and black – the color of the latter – will be effectively removed."

The inheritance of skin color differs from the inheritance of eye color, for example. In the latter there are dominant and recessive genes. Simply stated, if one dark eye color gene and one light eye color gene couple together, the dark one dominates and the effect is the same as if both were dark. The light eye color gene is recessive and can manifest itself in future generations. The inheritance of skin color, however, works on an entirely different principle. When a dark skin color gene and a light skin color gene couple together, the result is a blending of the two. It has been seen that as long as subsequent generations of mulattoes of any degree continue to mate with whites, the skin color of each new generation will necessarily be lighter. Even in cases where white people have remote black ancestry, it is impossible to produce a genetic throwback because dark skin color genes have all been blended out.

The issue of skin color inheritance has had an interesting history that can be traced back over 2,000 years to ancient times. To begin with, it must be understood that in those days, there was no racial prejudice per se. Unlike America, nowhere in the entire classical world was there ever any law which forbid intermarriage based on skin color or race. The Roman statesman and philosopher Cicero (106-43 B.C.) discussed the commonalities which exist among all people and asserted that "there is no difference in race....Nor is there anyone of any race who has taken nature as his guide that cannot reach virtue." The antipathy which did exist in ancient society was that of xenophobia, a fear of strangers or foreigners, including those of different cultures or religions. The dislike that Spartans and Cretans felt for strangers, for example, was well known as was the religious intolerance expressed toward Jews and Christians with their belief in monotheism. With no racial prejudice and no prohibitive social stigma attached to skin color, interracial sexual relations occurred freely throughout the ancient world. The Roman emperor Lucius Septimius Severus, an African, married Julia Domna, a white woman (PLATE 4). Ancient interracial sexuality can also be seen in works of art (PLATES 5, 6, 7) and in literature written by white men who were sexually attracted to black women. The Greek poet and epigrammatist Asclepiades of Samos (fl. third century B.C.) wrote:

> When looking at her beauty I melt as wax does before the fire. She is black but what is that to me? Coals are black, but when lit they shine as bright as roses.

The Roman epigrammatist Martial (fl. first century A.D.) expressed:

> A certain girl who is whiter than a washed swan wants me. She is whiter than silver, snow, a lily, or a privet. But I desire a girl I could name who is blacker than night, an ant, pitch, a jackdaw, or a cicada.

With interracial marriage not thought of as anything extraordinary, a white woman having a mulatto child was uneventful. Problems arose, however, when a white woman who was married to a white man had a mulatto child. The Roman poet Ovid (43 B.C.-?17 A.D.) alludes to adultery in a story from Roman mythology where white Aurora and white Tithonus produce a black son (which could only happen in mythology):

> A black son was born to you, the color of his mother's heart. I might wish that Tithonus could talk about you. No woman would ever be more morally disgraced in heaven.

In the real world, women who cheated on their husbands had a great deal to worry about because *adultery* was considered an offense so severe as to be *punishable by death*. The words of Roman statesman Marcus Porcius Cato (234-149 B.C.) say it all:

> When a husband divorces his wife...he judges the woman as a censor would, and has full powers if

> she has been guilty of any wrong or shameful act;
> she is severely punished if she has drunk wine; if
> she has done wrong with another man she is
> condemned to death. [Furthermore, the hus-
> band can carry out the execution himself! Cato
> writes,] If you should take your wife in adultery,
> you may with impunity put her to death without
> a trial; but if you should commit adultery or
> indecency, she must not presume to lay a finger
> on you, nor does the law permit it.

White women married to white men were giving birth to mulatto babies and being charged with adultery. To admit the obvious would be to admit the offense, so other explanations were sought in order to maintain the innocence of the women so charged. Two popular theories evolved – *atavism* and *maternal impression.*

The Greek philosopher Aristotle (384-322 B.C.) began the tradition of interracial atavism, explaining that the black [mulatto] son of a white woman was a hereditary throwback to the child's grandfather:

> Children can resemble their more remote an-
> cestors....There was at Elis a woman who co-
> habited with a Negro. Her daughter was not a
> Negro, but the son that came from that daughter
> was.

Aristotle's explanation provided a powerful answer. Greek author Antigonus of Carystus (fl. 250 B.C.) and Greek scholar Aristophanes of Byzantium (257?-?180 B.C.) both incorporated Aristotle's account into their own works. More than three centuries after Aristotle, this explanation was still popular. The Roman scholar Pliny (23-79 A.D.) wrote regarding oddities of birth:

> One certain example is that of the renowned
> boxer Nicaeus, born at Byzantium, whose
> mother was the daughter of adultery with a
> Negro. Her complexion was no different from
> that of the others [other white women], but her
> son Nicaeus appeared like his Negro grand-
> father.

PLATE 4

Family Portrait of
LUCIUS SEPTIMIUS SEVERUS - Roman emperor (193-211 A.D.)
painting on wood roundel

PLATE 5

ANCIENT GREEK POTTERY (late sixth century B.C.)
white woman/black man

PLATE 6

Painting from Pompeii (mid-first century A.D.)
POLYPHEMUS AND GALATEA
two figures from ancient mythology illustrated in this
particular example as a black male and a white female

PLATE 7

Mosaic and details
ROMAN INTERRACIAL COUPLE (third/fourth century A.D.)
from Tunisia

The seemingly impossible birth which Aristotle described was not a throwback and is easily explained otherwise. The white woman from Elis was pregnant with a baby fathered by a *white* man. When her daughter was born, she was, of course, white. That daughter's son, who was expected to be white but was not, was fathered by a *black* man. Likewise, Nicaeus' white grandmother may have committed adultery with a Negro, but her daughter, Nicaeus' mother, was white because she was fathered by a white man. Her son Nicaeus, however, was fathered by a black man.

Greek biographer and commentator Plutarch (46?-?120 A.D.), a contemporary of Pliny, presented an even more abstract example of atavism:

> A certain Greek woman, on bearing a black child
> and being charged with adultery, discovered that
> there was a Negro in her family four generations
> back.

Aristotle, his followers, Pliny, and Plutarch all promoted atavism. In ancient times, this theory was one way of explaining how a white woman could have a black (but really mulatto) baby even though she was married to a white man, without being an adulteress.

Maternal impression was the other technique used to account for how a so-called black baby could be born to two white parents. Pliny explained the general theory as follows:

> A great many likenesses that appear accidental
> were influenced by sense impressions of sights
> and sounds received at the time of conception. A
> trivial thought suddenly crossing the mind of
> either parent will also produce likeness.

It was believed that at the moment of conception the mind of the white woman was influenced by a mere thought of a black man, so that somehow an impression was left upon her and she produced a "black" child. Roman rhetorician Calpurnius Flaccus (fl. second century A.D.) discussed pro and con views of maternal impression in his declamation *Negro Birth*. On one hand, "Each people keeps its own appearance....The types of mortal men are diverse, yet no one is dissimilar to his own people." On the other hand, presumably under the influence of maternal impression, the dark color of the child may be explained as "skin scorched by imperfection of the blood." Doctor of the Church Saint Jerome (340?-420) explained, "Nor is it strange that this is the nature of women in their conceiving, namely that they beget the kind of offspring which they see or they conceive in their minds in the extreme heat of passion." Saint Jerome relates how by using this argument the Roman rhetorician Quintilian (fl. first century A.D.) defended a Roman matron who gave birth to a black [mulatto] child.

Apparently, in ancient times it was not uncommon to have sexually suggestive paintings on bedroom walls (like PLATE 6, for example), and such art work provided a ready explanation for maternal impression. Saint Augustine (354-430), church father and philosopher, stated that an account is to be found written in the books of the Greek physician Hippocrates (460?-?377 B.C.) in which a woman was suspected of adultery when she produced a very beautiful child who was dissimilar to either parent or family. She was freed from suspicion when it was determined that she had been influenced by a certain painting in her room. The original account of Hippocrates is not to be found in his extant works and is assumed lost, however, whether true or not, the fact is that Saint Augustine perpetuated the concept of maternal impression by including it in his own writings. The story was carried into three fifteenth-century manuscripts which advanced the view still further. In the words of researcher Lynn Thorndike, each describes a white woman who "as a result of fixing her gaze upon the picture of a Negro at the time of conception, gave birth to a child as black as the figure in the picture." These particular reports deal with the double genetic impossibilities of maternal impression and two white people producing a black child. It is worth noting that the idea of maternal impression was not limited exclusively to white women. In the fictional tale *Aethiopia,* an early Greek romance by Heliodorus (fourth century? A.D.), the black queen Persinna who is married to a black husband gives birth to a white daughter and believes that at the time of conception she was looking at a picture of Andromeda, a white woman.

Atavism and maternal impression have had a mixed history of acceptance and rejection. One proponent of atavism was phrenologist O. S. Fowler who recorded this interesting case in 1843:

> Two white parents in New Jersey, were very
> much astonished to find in their child unequiv-

> ocal marks of the African race and blood....His
> wife protested her innocence in terms so strong
> and solemn, that he was finally led to believe in
> her integrity. Still, no explanation of the phenom-
> enon appeared. At length he sailed for France,
> and visited a town on its frontiers where her
> family had resided for several generations, and
> found, to his joy, that his wife's *great grandfather*
> was an African.

The idea of atavism has survived into modern times. In 1972, for
example, sociologist Ian Robertson and commentator Phillip
Whitten reported that some whites in South Africa still utilize "the
genetic throwback" to account for a mulatto birth to white parents.
As explained earlier in this chapter, interracial atavism is a genetic
impossibility. Even so, the concept endures. Maternal impression,
on the other hand, appears not to have survived. Although modern
examples are lacking, it was a popular concept in the past. Unlike
other references already cited, English author Reginald Scot knew
that maternal impression was outright fraud and spoke the truth back
in 1584:

> A woman that brought forth a young Negro, by
> means of an old Negro who was in her house at
> the time of her conception, whom she beheld in
> fantasy, as is supposed...a jealous husband will
> not be satisfied with such fantastical imagina-
> tions. For in truth a Negro never faileth to beget
> black children, of what colour soever the other
> be.

In other cases, however, maternal impression was shown to be
valid, acceptable, and popular. Richard Brathwait, English poet and
author (1641):

> It is incredible, what rare effects were sometimes
> drawn from a *Negro Picture,* being onely hung
> up in a Ladies Chamber.

In the early 1700s the Dutch physician Hermann Boerhaave related,

> A Princess was delivered of a black daughter, by

> only seeing, for the first time, a Negro whilst she
> was pregnant.

In London *The Morning Post, and Daily Advertiser* of December 22, 1786 alluded to maternal impression in the following statement about mulattoes:

> The numerous dingy-coloured [dusky] faces
> which crowded our streets, must have their
> origin in our wives being *terrified* when preg-
> nant, by the numerous Africans who were to be
> seen in all parts of the town.

While traveling in South Africa in the 1830s, Sir James Edward Alexander visited with a white couple who after seven months of marriage had a mulatto child. According to the husband,

> One day his wife was going out and was fright-
> ened by a black man, whom she suddenly saw
> behind the door, and that the child became
> black in consequence.

Maternal impression was so widely accepted that reports of the phenomenon even appeared in a prestigious French medical journal in 1873. One case concerned a woman who had had carnal relations many times with a black in America. On returning to Europe she was placed in a convent, and after a stay of two years she left and married a white man. After nine months of pregnancy she gave birth to a black infant.

In several of the preceding accounts as well as others in this chapter, the word "black" was used figuratively to mean mulatto. A New York court case which occurred in 1816 exemplifies how confusing such usage can be. The court reviewed forty-year-old records wherein it was found that a white woman named Catreen Race had "delivered of a male black child" and claimed that a white man named Adam Heydon was the father. The court acknowledged that white women could produce mulatto children but not black ones and stated that if "Catreen Race, a white woman, had been delivered of a mulatto child, instead of a black child, there could be no question on the subject of illegitimacy, because it would have appeared impossible for Adam Heydon, a white man, to have been the father." However, Catreen Race produced a black baby (on paper, at least) and not a mulatto, and the court ruled that Adam Heydon was the father, implying that atavism or maternal impression was responsible. What had to have happened was that Catreen Race did have a mulatto child, but the court mistakenly interpreted the forty-year-old records and took the word "black" to mean Negro rather than the general figurative term for a mulatto. (For another example of a white woman's mulatto baby who was referred to as black, see Chapter 5, p. 85.) A related court case is worth mentioning here. In 1840 a Virginia court appropriately ruled in agreement with "professional men that, according to the course of nature, a mulatto child cannot be the offspring of two white persons."

For over 2,000 years atavism and maternal impression were ways of explaining how a white woman married to a white man could give birth to a mulatto (often referred to as a black) child. In looking back over this span of time, it is really remarkable how these two ideas have flourished. As science has evolved and more accurate information has become available in the fields of genetics and heredity, knowledge has replaced ignorance, and this long history is now finally drawing to a close.

Chapter 7.   HOW DO WE INHERIT OUR SKIN COLOR?

Louis Levine, *Biology of the Gene,* 2d ed. (St. Louis, 1973), 82 concerning skin color genes and potency; George Best, "A True Discourse of the Three Voyages of Discoverie," in *The Principal Navigations, Voyages, Traffiques & Discoveries of the English Nation,* comp. Richard Hakluyt (N. Y., 1904), 7:262 ("Ethiopian," an archaic general term for Negro, in original.)

For skin color inheritance, see L. C. Dunn and Th. Dobzhansky, *Heredity, Race and Society* (N. Y., New American Library, 1952), 58-61; Carroll Lane Fenton, *Our Living World* (Garden City, 1953), 195; Max Levitan and Ashley Montagu, *Textbook of Human Genetics* (N. Y., 1971), 635; Amram Scheinfeld, *Heredity in Humans* (N. Y., 1972), 57, 59; Laurence H. Snyder, *The Principles of Heredity* (N. Y., 1935), 127; A. M. Winchester and Thomas R. Mertens, *Human Genetics,* 4th ed. (Columbus, 1983), 66. For an example of modern misinformation, see Julian S. Huxley and A. C. Haddon, *We Europeans: A Survey of "Racial" Problems* (N. Y., 1936), 61.

Curt Stern refers to "the dark skin of many Mediterranean whites," and such a white and a nearly white mulatto could have a child darker than the nearly white due to "minor modifying alleles." Concerning whites in general, however, Stern goes on to say that "since the genetic basis of skin-color differences is not established beyond doubt, it would be unscientific to deny the possibility that, in marriages of white and near-whites, children somewhat darker than their near-white parent could be produced." *Principles of Human Genetics,* 3d ed. (San Francisco, 1973), 445, 448. While the first case is true, the second case is false and Stern's view is unnecessarily cautious. Inasmuch as the white parent can only contribute light skin color genes and the nearly white parent can only contribute mostly light skin color genes, even if their child received *all* of the dark skin color genes from the nearly white parent, how could the child be *darker* than its nearly white parent? Furthermore, in the professional literature on genetics and skin color inheritance, not one such case has ever been reported!

Regarding the twins, see D. M. Cheers, "A Visit with Unusual Twins," *Jet* 70 (June 2, 1986): 30-32; D. Michael Cheers, "Britain's Most Amazing Twins," *Ebony* 39 (April 1984): 42+; "A Genetic

Puzzle," *Ebony* 36 (December 1980): 80+.

The census reference may be had in Kenneth M. Stampp, *The Peculiar Institution: Slavery in the Ante-Bellum South* (N. Y., Vintage Books, 1956), 351 n. 9.

Marquis de Chastellux, *Travels in North America in the Years 1780, 1781 and 1782,* ed. and trans. Howard C. Rice, Jr. (Chapel Hill, 1963), 2:440-41; "Philo Humanitas," (letter to the editor), *Genius of Universal Emancipation,* ed. and pub. Benjamin Lundy (Greeneville, Tenn.), 3 (Ninth Month 1823): 42 (italics in original); [William Gilmore Simms], *Slavery in America, Being a Brief Review of Miss Martineau on That Subject* (Richmond, 1838), 40. This pamphlet was published anonymously, however, the 1852 version appeared with the author's name. The quotation cited on page 40 of the former is noticeably absent from the latter. W. Gilmore Simms, *The Morals of Slavery,* in *The Pro-Slavery Argument* (1852; reprint, N. Y., 1968), 230.

Regarding eye color being Mendelian, see Victor A. McKusick, *Mendelian Inheritance in Man,* 8th ed. (Baltimore, 1988), 925-26, and Scheinfeld, *Heredity,* chap. 7.

In the ancient world, marriage prohibitions were based on social class. In Rome the Twelve Tables (449 B.C.) outlawed intermarriage between plebeians (commoners) and patricians (aristocrats). The Canuleian Law (445 B.C.), however, reversed this policy and permitted such intermarriages. The Julian Law on Classes Permitted to Marry (18 B.C.) stated that with the exception of senators, their children, grandchildren, and great grandchildren, all free men could marry free women providing they were not women of ill repute. Naphtali Lewis and Meyer Reinhold, eds., *Roman Civilization* (N. Y., 1951, 1955), 1:109, 112-13 and 2:50-52. The Athenian statesman Pericles had a law passed in 451/0 B.C. which only legitimized marriage between two Athenian citizens. Aubrey Diller, *Race Mixture Among the Greeks Before Alexander* (Westport, 1971), 91, 123, 136-37, 152-59. Alexander the Great, on the other hand, encouraged intermarriage between Greeks and barbarians. Simon Davis, *Race-Relations in Ancient Egypt: Greek, Egyptian, Hebrew, Roman* (London, 1953), 10, 12, and also 54, 69. In addition, see *Encyclopaedia of the Social Sciences,* s.v. "Intermarriage"; Frank M. Snowden, Jr., *Blacks in Antiquity: Ethiopians in the Greco-Roman Experience* (Cambridge, Mass., 1970), 169 and his companion volume

Before Color Prejudice: The Ancient View of Blacks (Cambridge, Mass., 1983).

Cicero *On Laws* 1.10.30, also *Pro Balbo* 22.51. Regarding xenophobia, see Davis, *Race-Relations,* xv, xvii, 113-32, 151-65; Diller, *Race Mixture,* 22-23, 32, 71-73; John Gill, *Notices of the Jews and Their Country by the Classic Writers of Antiquity* (1872; reprint, Westport, 1976); Simeon L. Guterman, *Religious Toleration and Persecution in Ancient Rome* (London, 1951); A. N. Sherwin-White, *Racial Prejudice in Imperial Rome* (Cambridge, Eng., 1967), 1, 60, 66, 86-101. For the Spartan and Cretan references, see W. K. Lacey, *The Family in Classical Greece* (Ithaca, 1968), 200, 208.

Concerning the skin color of Septimius Severus, a family portrait which has survived speaks for itself. Severus was born in Leptis Magna, North Africa. Caius Pescennius Niger, a peer of Severus who challenged him for the title of emperor, also has been considered black because his cognomen of Niger means "black" in Latin. In the biography of Niger by Aelius Spartianus, however, he is described as having a white body with a ruddy face, and a black neck which was said to account for his name. "Pescennius Niger," in *Scriptores Historiae Augustae* 6.5-6. Africans were great religious leaders as well. Relatively unknown but true nonetheless, there were three African popes – Victor (fl. late second century), Miltiades (311-314), and Gelasius (492-496). *The Book of the Popes (Liber Pontificalis),* trans. Louise Ropes Loomis (1916; reprint, N. Y., 1965), 17-19, 40-41, 110-14.

Mythical male deities and satyrs were depicted with deep bronze complexions in some instances. For examples of this treatment, see Daedalus and Pan in Theodore H. Feder, ed., *Great Treasures of Pompeii & Herculaneum* (N. Y., 1978), 89, 137, and satyrs in Michael Grant et al., *Eros in Pompeii: The Secret Rooms of the National Museum of Naples* (N. Y., 1975), 145, 162, 163. Mortal (white) men have also been depicted with dark complexions as in Grant et al., *Eros,* 33, 36, and even 153, but never as dark as 152, the male in PLATE 6. The color of this black figure (identified as the mythical Polyphemus) closely resembles that of the priests officiating a ceremony for the goddess Isis. See Frank M. Snowden, Jr., "Iconographical Evidence on the Black Populations in Greco-Roman Antiquity," in *The Image of the Black in Western Art 1:*

From the Pharaohs to the Fall of the Roman Empire (N. Y., 1976), figure 222, and text on 221, 224.

Asclepiades of Samos, in *Greek Anthology* 5.210; Martial *The Epigrams* 1.115. Also for example, Ovid *The Loves* 2.5.39-40, and Propertius *The Elegies* 2.26.41-42.

Ovid *The Loves* 1.13.33-36. Commentaries may be had in Hermann Fränkel, *Ovid: A Poet between Two Worlds* (Berkeley, 1969), 14-15, 178-79, and J. C. McKeown, *Ovid: Amores: Text, Prolegomena and Commentary* (Leeds, Eng., 1989), 2:355-58. The Roman lawyer and satirist Juvenal (60?-?140 A.D.) ridicules interracial adultery in *Satires* 6.597-601. Cato quoted in Lewis and Reinhold, *Roman Civilization* 1:508, and also see 60. Of course, misogyny did not begin in ancient Rome. For references to misogyny in the Bible, see Katherine M. Rogers, *The Troublesome Helpmate: A History of Misogyny in Literature* (Seattle, Washington Paperback, 1968), 3-22.

Aristotle *On the Generation of Animals* 1.18.722a and *History of Animals* 7.6.586a; Antigonus of Carystus *Collections of Amazing Histories* 112 (122), in *Rerum Naturalium Scriptores Graeci Minores,* ed. Otto Keller (Leipzig, 1877); Aristophanes of Byzantium *Summary of the History of Animals* 2.272, in *Supplementum Aristotelicum* 1:pt. 1, ed. Spyridon P. Lambros (Berlin, 1885); Pliny *Natural History* 7.12.51; Plutarch *On the Late Vengeance of Divinity* 21.563 (in *Moralia,* Book 7).

Pliny *Natural History* 7.12.52; Calpurnius Flaccus *Declamationes 2 (Bibliotheca Classica Latina,* 80: 523-26); Saint Jerome *Hebrew Questions in the Book of Genesis* 30, 32.33 *(Corpus Christianorum, Series Latina,* 72.38) and *Quintiliani quae feruntur Declamationes XIX maiores,* ed. G. Lehnert (Leipzig, 1905), 353.

Regarding erotic paintings on bedroom walls, Antonio De Simone and Maria Teresa Merella who are affiliated with the National Archaeological Museum of Naples state that "these little paintings may have functioned as a sort of figurative grammar of love, and may have been intended as visual enticements to make love. Many have in fact been found not only in brothels but also in the bedrooms of private houses, as if they were private collections of erotic art." Grant et al., *Eros,* 154.

Saint Augustine *Questions in Genesis* 93 *(Corpus Christianorum, Series Latina,* 33.35). Also, see Laurent Joubert, *Treatise on*

Laughter (1579; reprint, trans. Gregory David de Rocher, University, Al., 1980), 67, and *The Collected Works of Ambroise Paré. Translated Out of the Latin by Thomas Johnson* (1634 from the 1579 ed.; reprint, Pound Ridge, N. Y., 1968), 978. The woodcut used by Paré to portray his prose also served as the model for illustrations which appeared later in many English and American editions of *Aristotle's Masterpiece* (titles vary), an early work on human sexuality. Also, for examples of text references to maternal impression, see *Aristotle's Compleat Master Piece,* 1749 edition, 90, and *Aristotle's Book of Problems,* 1776 edition, 65. (These 2 reprinted and bound with others in 1 vol. by Garland Publishing [N. Y., 1986].) Lynn Thorndike, "De Complexionibus," *Isis* 49 (December 1958): 399-400 ("Ethiopian" in original); Heliodorus *Aethiopia* 4.8.

O. S. Fowler, *Hereditary Descent: Its Laws and Facts, Illustrated and Applied to the Improvement of Mankind* (N. Y., 1843), 34-35 (italics in original); Ian Robertson and Phillip Whitten, "Sexual Politics in South Africa," *Progressive* 36 (September 1972): 44; Reginald Scot, *The Discoverie of Witchcraft* (1584; reprint, Carbondale, Ill., 1964), 262 ("blacke Moore" in original); Richard Brathwait, *The English Gentlewoman,* 3d ed. (London, 1641), 354 ("Morian" and italics in original); Boerhaave cited in Nathaniel Wanley, *The Wonders of the Little World,* 6 books in 1 vol. (London, 1774), 2:106 ("blackmoor" in original); *The Morning Post, and Daily Advertiser,* 22 Dec. 1786, p. 2 (italics in original); James Edward Alexander, *An Expedition of Discovery into the Interior of Africa* (London, 1838), 1:77; *Bulletin de la Société Médicale de la Suisse Romande* 7 (August 1873): 241. Also, see *The Works of Sir Thomas Browne,* ed. Geoffrey Keyes (London, 1928), 2:466-67, and Don Cameron Allen, *The Legend of Noah: Renaissance Rationalism in Art, Science, and Letters* (Urbana, 1963), 119. For a tongue in cheek example of maternal impression, see Harold M. Hyman, "Election of 1864," in *History of American Presidential Elections, 1789-1968,* ed. Arthur M. Schlesinger, Jr. et al. (N. Y., 1971), 2:1231.

Helen Tunnicliff Catterall, ed., *Judicial Cases Concerning American Slavery and the Negro* (1926; reprint, N. Y., 1968), 4:370, and also 2:136; 1:196.

8

WHAT'S THE ATTRACTION?

Of the white women in the national probability sample, 27% agreed with the belief that many white women have fantasized about a sexual experience with an Afro-American man (Belief Statement 7). Less overtly sexual was the belief about dating, and here 65% agreed that if there were no social pressures against it, a white woman would date an Afro-American man if she wanted to (Belief Statement 8).

The first impression a woman has when she looks at a man is his *appearance.* Before words are ever exchanged, a visual perception is made. There are attractive and not so attractive men throughout the entire world regardless of their skin color, and a white woman may be initially drawn to a black man because she finds him attractive as a man, a member of the opposite sex. It is reasonable to suggest that in some instances, such initial attraction may result in sexual fantasy. Although the professional literature contains much on the subject of sexual fantasy in general, surprising but true nonetheless, it is virtually devoid of articles which deal specifically with interracial sexual fantasy. One preliminary study, however, can be mentioned. In 1974 Alan Daniel Davidson surveyed 202 unmarried undergraduate female students at the University of Cincinnati on the subject of sexual fantasy. One item included in his questionnaire was, "I have thought about making love to someone who is of a different race than I am." He found that 68.3% had the fantasy "occasionally" to "very often," and 21.8% had it "often" to "very often."

Popular paperbacks have addressed interracial sexual fantasy, but it is unfortunate that these fantasies tend to treat the black male involved solely as a potent sex object. As explained in Chapter 6, this myth of a black sexual superiority and its resultant sexual stereotype originated back in slavery days and has endured ever since. J. Aphrodite (pseud.) included an interracial sexual fantasy about a white woman and a black man in her collection of fantasies, and although pornographic in nature and hardly worth mentioning in and of itself, she followed it with an editorial comment that is particularly noteworthy:

> Since *To Turn You On* was written by a woman for women, it was not designed to please males. A few did have a chance to read the original script. If they objected to anything, invariably it was to the story you've just shared. They were offended. They were angered. They were indignant. "No woman could have such a fantasy," was their theme. If only for that reason, I marked it a "must include." Men have been dictating women's fantasies far too long!

Indeed, it would be interesting to know the extent to which white men believe that white women fantasize about black men being sexually "superior." Be that as it may, it is important to recall from the survey findings that only a small number of white women really believe any sexual difference exists at all (Belief Statement 4).

As recently as 1967, sixteen states had laws on their books forbidding interracial marriage. Such marriages, although now legal, are still not readily acceptable in society at large, and it is fair to say that many American white women have grown up with the knowledge that prejudice exists against black people whether they themselves are prejudiced or not. What motivational dynamics are in force which allow a white woman to override this negativity and accept being attracted to the "forbidden"?

Professor Alvin F. Poussaint of Harvard University has suggested that the "forbidden fruit syndrome," while still present, is much less so today than even a generation ago. He credits the woman's liberation movement for much of this change in thinking. Psychiatrist Ludwig Eidelberg views the attraction of the forbidden in psychoanalytic terms. Simply stated, he believes that such behavior in general (in a literally sexual context or otherwise) simultaneously satisfies our sex drive and our aggressive instincts. Likewise, psychoanalyst Amelie Oksenberg Rorty has pointed out that "wherever there is a strong social prohibition on the expression of a drive or an activity, we may presume that there is a strong tendency, perhaps with the force of an instinctual drive, to perform that activity." In light of the vicissitudes of human experience, perhaps the desire for variety is also somehow related to being attracted to the forbidden.

Psychoanalysis explains the sexual attraction a white woman may experience toward a black man in terms of the Oedipus complex, so named after Oedipus, the King of Thebes in Greek mythology who unwittingly killed his father and married his mother. The Oedipus complex was originally conceived of by Sigmund Freud who made reference to the psychological aspects extant in the child-mother-father interaction. Not only did Freud himself revise the concept over the years, but many of his followers have argued over debatable points and have reassessed its inner dynamics, thereby establishing new and various interpretations. Consensus is even lacking regarding the term itself with some preferring "Electra complex" when used specifically with reference to females.

Although the Oedipus complex is an involved psychoanalytic construct, particularly in its technical aspects, its basic tenets are not difficult to understand. Between the ages of about three to five, a little girl finds her father to be a love object and her mother competition for her father's love. Mother is viewed as a rival standing in the way of desired emotional gratification with father. Aggression is transferred to mother and attraction is attached to father. As she strives to become her own separate individual, a little girl detaches from mother as her primary love object and father takes on that role, particularly if he is emotionally close and supportive. In a healthy environment, this situation resolves itself by the time the girl is four or five years old. The Oedipus complex becomes recrudescent again at the time of puberty. As a young sexually viable female, she now represses any sexual feelings she may have toward her father. Awareness of his enjoyment of her growth and development encourages her to share like interests and pastimes with him, thereby desexualizing the relationship and allowing psychosexual development to proceed unimpeded. Oedipal problems occur for the girl when there is a failure to identify with her mother and feminine identity or when she has been unable to successfully integrate the sexual components of the love for her father. *The manner in which she has transacted with these Oedipal conflicts will play a major role in her later love relationships.* If anxieties experienced go unresolved, the girl may become fixated at this stage of her emotional development and may go through life *unconsciously* seeking a repetition of the Oedipal situation, longing for her father and resenting her mother. As psychiatrist Edith Jacobson has said, "The final outcome of her conflict depends a great deal on the father's attitudes and on the mother's personality and love." The father's attitude toward his daughter's puberty is of particular importance.*

A resolved Oedipus complex leaves a girl with an idealized image of her father which unconsciously influences how she feels about men who share common qualities with him; she was accepted by her father and can feel accepted by men like him. On the other hand, in the absence of satisfactory bonding with her father, a girl may grow up feeling unloved and by extension incapable of male acceptance. With the onset of womanhood, sexual behavior is found to be one means by which she *can* be accepted by men; however, unable to use this sexuality to gain her real father's acceptance, she seeks the love she is looking for from "daddy" in the arms of other men – substitute father figures. Experiencing sex with men who are like her father results in guilt because the unconscious desire to make love with (and thereby gain acceptance from) her real father is still present and making its influence known. This conflict is circumvented by choosing men who are *unlike* her father. According to this psychoanalytic interpretation, a woman with an unresolved Oedipus complex will unconsciously seek out interethnic and/or interfaith sexual relationships in order to fulfill this criterion of *different*. Interracial sexual relationships extend that difference yet one more dimension to skin color. For those white women who manifest their unresolved Oedipus complex interracially, a black man can not be conceived of as a substitute father figure because even though he may possess personality traits like those of her father, other father-

---

* Setting the Oedipus complex aside for a moment and speaking in general, there is an important observation to be made here. At this stage in their daughters' development, some fathers feel awkward or uncomfortable and distance themselves from their daughters when they change from little girls into young women. Unknown to the father, this may prove devastating for a daughter who once being close to her father now finds that her new body has driven him away. Many of these young women take this rejection personally and feel that they are physically unattractive because they cannot account for their fathers' change in behavior in any other way. Support and sensitivity from fathers are particularly important during this critical developmental stage.

qualities being identified within white men are not present in a man so different in cultural background and appearance. For these women, the sexual attraction to a black man is unconscious, and the sex act can be experienced without the guilt had in sex with white men who are like their father.

The existence of the Oedipus complex as well as its universality have been the subjects of countless books and articles in the professional literature. The battle lines have been drawn. Many authorities believe that the Oedipus complex really exists and just as many do not. Problems of definition compound the issue further. Numerous texts in the social sciences describe what appears to be the intrafamilial dynamics that characterize the Oedipus complex (particularly the aggression transferred to the same-sex parent) but do not refer to the term itself. Moreover, the original construct as delineated by Freud has undergone so many changes, revisions, and modifications that it is hardly recognizable. Surely, the familial components of child-mother-father do exist and are universal, but whether or not they fit into the Freudian schema particularly or universally continues to be debated.

As stated previously, attractive men are attractive regardless of their skin color. Rather than attribute interracial sexual attraction to something in the realm of the mysterious and the unknowable, can it be said that a white woman is initially attracted to a black man just as she is to a white man simply because she sees that he is a good-looking man? Whatever the explanation, a white woman who finds a black man attractive may date him. Interracial dating has been going on for decades.

National data concerning interracial dating have been published which include the views of "whites" and "women," but not "white women." *Newsweek Magazine* reported that in 1963 (a time when interracial marriage was still against the law in many states), 90% of all whites surveyed "would mind" if their "teen-age child dated a Negro." Likewise, the figure for 1966 was 88%. In 1965 Louis Harris found that 92% of all whites surveyed "would object" to their "own daughter dating a Negro," and in 1969 with the wording changed to "own teenage child," 83% would be "concerned." *Life Magazine* commissioned a Louis Harris poll in 1971 which found that "almost one American in five has had a date with someone outside his or her race." The number was one out of every three for those 21 to 25 years old. With these figures in mind, it was interesting that 55% of the total sample (women, men, whites, blacks) did not "even *know* anyone who has dated interracially." Among other findings, 28% approved of interracial dating for their own children while 25% forbid it. In what might well be considered the bottom line in the Louis Harris poll, 77% agreed, "No matter what older people and parents say, young people of different races are going to see each other socially and we'd better get used to it."

The so-called Sorensen Report (1973) on teenage sexuality in America focused in on a national probability sample of 411 adolescents. Three statements in Sorensen's questionnaire were concerned with interracial sexuality. First, "I don't think that I would want to have sex with a person of another race." Of all the girls (combined white and nonwhite) surveyed, 60% of those 13 to 15 years old and 53% of those 16 to 19 responded with "True." Second, "A white girl and a black boy having sex together is something that I would consider immoral, even if both of them wanted to do it." Here 37% of the younger group and 27% of the older group responded with "True." When the second statement was reversed, "A white boy and a black girl having sex together...", the figures were 40% and 28% respectively. In addition to interracial sex, the Sorensen Report addressed other issues which it chose to judge as possibly having an immoral component. Among the teenagers surveyed, however, the two statements which posed interracial sex as being immoral ranked among those with the lowest amount of agreement. Another survey which included the subject of interracial sexual relations was published in the October, 1989 issue of *Seventeen Magazine*. Out of 1,023 young women 14 to 21 years old, 31% of those who responded agreed with the statement, "I would marry someone of a different race." In regard to dating, however, a somewhat higher agreement rate of 40% was obtained for the statement, "I would go out with someone of another race." Janet Bode (1989) interviewed teenagers who dated interracially or cross-culturally and reported, "The teen couples I talked to mentioned the sense of isolation they sometimes feel." Apparently, many such teenagers experience degrees of social distancing from those not approving of their behavior.

In the research on interracial dating, only two small-scale studies include data specifically regarding white women. Charles V. Willie and Joan D. Levy surveyed approximately 200 white students in 1969 and 1970 "on the campuses of four predominantly white colleges in upstate New York." Their results showed that 45% of the white women respondents dated interracially. Philip A. Belcastro (1985) used a sample of undergraduates "from a large midwestern university" who were enrolled in health education courses and found that 90.4% of the 251 white women surveyed had never experienced "interracial coitus."

Closely related to interracial dating is the issue of interracial marriage. As was true for interracial dating, national data concerning interracial marriage have also been published, but once again, white women as a group were not specifically included. Nonetheless, even in terms of "whites" and "women" the data are still of interest. *Newsweek* reported that in 1963, 84% of all whites surveyed "would mind" if their "close friend or relative married a Negro." In 1966 the figure was 79%. The Gallup Organization has conducted a series of surveys which show a positive trend toward the acceptance of interracial marriage. In 1972, 25% of all whites surveyed approved of marriage between whites and nonwhites. In 1978 the approval rate rose to 32% for all whites, and the figure for all women (white and nonwhite) was 35%. In 1983 the wording of the survey question was changed from "whites and nonwhites" to "blacks and whites," and approval rates rose yet again to 38% for all whites and 41% for all women (white and nonwhite). These data are certainly significant, especially when considered in light of long-term direction. It must be noted, however, that whenever survey data are presented in terms of "women," white women and black women (or white women and nonwhite women as the case may be) have been combined together and the opinions of each as separate components of society go unrepresented as a consequence. An excellent example which illustrates the need to separate out population components is to be found in published data for the 1974 "Virginia Slims American Women's Opinion Poll." When asked about the acceptance of a daughter "marrying someone of another race," 44% of the white women surveyed would "not accept it and have [a] strained relationship" with their daughter compared to only a 16% response rate for black women

(52% of the white women and 62% of the black women would "find it acceptable" or "accept but be unhappy about it"). In terms of a strained family relationship, the difference in data between white women and black women is very significant. If the data were presented in terms of "women" only, it is easy to see how the black perspective would be totally misrepresented.

Statistics from the U. S. Bureau of the Census have shown a steady rise in the rate of interracial marriages. The 1960 decennial census showed 25,496 marriages between white women and black men (and as of 1960 there were still twenty-two states which had laws against interracial marriage on their books). In 1970 the figure was 41,223, and by 1980 the number had more than doubled at 93,660. The March 1988 Current Population Survey, a different U. S. census survey and the latest to date, estimated the number of marriages between white women and black men at 149,000 (the 1980 figure in this series was 122,000). Interracial marriages between white men and black women have also been on the rise recently. The 1960 decennial census showed 25,913 such marriages, followed by 23,566 in 1970, and 27,329 in 1980. The March 1988 Current Population Survey estimated the number of marriages between white men and black women at 69,000 (the 1980 figure in this series was 45,000).

Interracial dating and interracial marriage may be on the rise, but there is still a social bias against them. Not surprisingly, such a bias has been reflected in college textbooks that present information about marriage and the family. Marie Ferguson Peters, a child development and family relations professional, has observed that this subject has been handled as a "deviant form of White American marriage" in many such texts, and that their authors often make unsubstantiated generalizations about caste and class. The manner in which interracial marriages have been treated in these college textbooks is symptomatic of the greater societal picture at large in which such marriages have been regarded as undesirable.

People who enter into interracial marriages are nonconformists who do not choose to adhere to the intraracial standard of contemporary social mores. Their nonconformity appears to be limited to the choice of their marriage partner, otherwise they appear to be rather conventional in terms of their marital motivations. Researcher Kris Jeter has studied the motives for intercultural and interracial marriage and has concluded, "The psychological dynamics for intermarriage are also found in 'straight' marriages. The bottom line is whether the union provides the necessary warmth, love, affection, excitement, caring, intimacy, and solidarity all human beings require." Ernest Porterfield, another researcher who has studied interracial marriage, stated, "In view of the greater opportunities for increased contacts and interaction between different groups in recent years, many interracial marriages now occur simply because the individuals are in love." When people are in situations where they have to interact with each other over time, the nearness tends to establish familiarity and promote acceptance. As sociologist George C. Homans stated back in 1950, "*Persons who interact frequently with one another tend to like one another.*" Such propinquity between whites and blacks, however, is not generally widespread, and it may be said that in many parts of the United States, interracial dating and interracial marriage are still found to elicit responses ranging anywhere from mere curiosity to utter disdain. In light of such responses, sexologists John Money and Anke A. Ehrhardt have observed, "The issue of miscegenation is so explosive that it can scarcely be mentioned in public and political discussion, perhaps because it is a foregone conclusion that black-white intermarriage will become routine." While statistics show that interracial marriages are on the increase, whether or not they will ultimately become "routine" remains to be seen.

Chapter 8.   WHAT'S THE ATTRACTION?

Alan Daniel Davidson, "The Relationship of Reported Sexual Daydreaming to Sexual Attitude, Sexual Knowledge, and Reported Sexual Experience in College Women" (Ph.D. diss., Univ. of Cincinnati, 1974), 82, 174. Also, see A. H. Maslow, "Self-Esteem (Dominance-Feeling) and Sexuality in Women," *Journal of Social Psychology* 16 (November, Second Half, 1942): 287. J. Aphrodite (pseud.), *To Turn You On: 39 Sex Fantasies for Women* (N. Y., Bantam, 1976), 199. Genre aside, the comments of Nancy Friday on the subject of interracial sexual fantasy are also worthy of consideration. *My Secret Garden: Women's Sexual Fantasies* (N. Y., 1973), 190-91. An earlier perspective on Friday's comments may be had in Helene Deutsch, *The Psychology of Women: A Psychoanalytic Interpretation* (1944; reprint, N. Y., 1971), 1:256.

Alvin F. Poussaint, "The Black Male-White Female, An Update," *Ebony* 38 (August 1983): 126; Ludwig Eidelberg, *Studies in Psychoanalysis* (N. Y., 1952), 135-36; Amelie Oksenberg Rorty, "Some Social Uses of the Forbidden," *Psychoanalytic Review* 58 (Winter 1971): 497; Donald W. Fiske and Salvatore R. Maddi, eds., *Functions of Varied Experience* (Homewood, Ill., 1961).

Sigmund Freud's idea of the Oedipus complex evolved over many years. In 1897 Freud wrote a letter to Wilhelm Fliess in which he described but did not formally name the Oedipus complex. Then in 1900 in *The Interpretation of Dreams,* Freud wrote, "Being in love with the one parent and hating the other are among the essential constituents of the stock of psychical impulses." In 1901 in *The Psychopathology of Everyday Life,* the wording "Oedipus dream" appears. Finally, in 1910, thirteen years after his original formulation, Freud used the term "Oedipus complex" in "A Special Type of Choice of Object Made by Men." *The Standard Edition of the Complete Psychological Works of Sigmund Freud,* trans. and ed. James Strachey (London, 1953-74), 1:265, 4:260-61, 6:178 n. 2, 11:171.

Perhaps the best general overview of Freud's initial ideas concerning the Oedipus complex is in Roy C. Calogeras and Fabian X. Schupper, "Origins and Early Formulations of the Oedipus Complex," *Journal of the American Psychoanalytic Association* 20 (October 1972): 751-75. For a synopsis of how the mature Oedipal formulation has been received by some of Freud's more notable followers, see Joel Paris, "The Oedipus Complex: A Critical Re-Examination," *Canadian Psychiatric Association Journal* 21 (no. 3, 1976): 173-79. Female sexuality in particular has been addressed in Sheila Hafter Gray, "The Resolution of the Oedipus Complex in Women," *Journal of the Philadelphia Association for Psychoanalysis* 3 (1976): 103-11; J. Lampl de Groot, "The Evolution of the Oedipus Complex in Women," *International Journal of Psycho-Analysis* 9 (July 1928): 332-45; Humberto Nagera, *Female Sexuality and the Oedipus Complex* (N. Y., 1975). Recent books on the Oedipus complex in general are George H. Pollock and John Munder Ross, eds., *The Oedipus Papers* (Madison, Conn., 1988), and Peter L. Rudnytsky, *Freud and Oedipus* (N. Y., 1987). An earlier treatment may be had in Patrick Mullahy, *Oedipus Myth and Complex: A Review of Psychoanalytic Theory* (N. Y., 1948). Edith Jacobson, *The Self and the Object World* (N. Y., 1973), 114.

It is unfortunate that the professional literature has tended to treat the interracial Oedipal dynamic solely in terms of *pathological* case studies. For a notable exception, see Walter F. Char, "Motivations for Intercultural Marriages," in *Adjustment in Intercultural Marriage,* ed. Wen-Shing Tseng et al. (Honolulu, 1977), 35-36. Of related interest, see Karl Abraham, *Clinical Papers and Essays on Psycho-Analysis* (N. Y., 1955), 2:21-28, 48-50; Karem Monsour, "Racial Prejudice and the Incest Taboo," *Psychiatric Annals* 2 (September 1972): 67.

The traditional Oedipal triangle of daughter(or son)-mother-father is often referred to in psychological literature, but with divorce a frequent occurrence in contemporary American society, many single-parent households exist where father visits or is absent altogether. How does this little girl or adolescent manifest her Oedipal psychosexual development? Clinical psychologist Lora Heims Tessman admonishes that if divorce occurs during the Oedipal period and the girl sees her father with a new woman, the impression is that father has chosen someone else and not her; that is, "a sense of rejection of her erotic feelings may become, for the daughter, an area of lifelong vulnerability....The intimacy the daughter desires, the fact that she sees it but is not part of it, may 'fix' it rigidly as a component of her wishes toward her father, which remain untransformed by the desexualizing influence of opportunities for further affectionate interaction." Psychologist E. Mavis Hetherington in her study of adolescent girls living with their mothers found that the girls with the most heterosexual problems had experienced father absence (due to death or divorce) before they were five years old – a significant Oedipal related finding.

Psychiatrist Peter B. Neubauer has written on the subject of one-parent children and concluded, "Fantasy objects, immensely idealized or endowed with terribly sadistic attributes, replacing an absent parent are nearly ubiquitous; their frequent occurrence in dynamically very different situations underlines their significance in the development of object relations." Of course, it must be said that whether the fantasy parent is idealized or sadistic will depend upon the qualities present in the child's general emotional environment, particularly the relationship with the existing parent.

It appears that a father figure whether real or imagined is necessary in the Oedipal phase of development. The difficulty for father-absent girls who compensate through fantasy is that the father figure remains a fantasized object. There are no opportunities for modification or illumination through life experience with an actual father, a love object with which to work through her Oedipal conflicts. Optimal psychosexual development for such a girl will depend in large part on finding a real male surrogate father figure with whom she can play out her role as if he were her real father. Such surrogates might include a male member of the extended family, for example.

L. H. Tessman, "A Note on the Father's Contribution to the Daughter's Ways of Loving and Working," in *Father and Child: Developmental and Clinical Perspectives,* ed. Stanley H. Cath et al. (Boston, 1982), 222; E. M. Hetherington, "Effects of Father Absence on Personality Development in Adolescent Daughters," *Developmental Psychology* 7 (November 1972): 324; P. B. Neubauer, "The One-Parent Child and His Oedipal Development," *Psychoanalytic Study of the Child* 15 (1960): 293. For more on fantasy fathers, see Anna Freud and Dorothy Burlingham, *Infants Without Families: Reports on the Hampstead Nurseries, 1939-1945,* vol. 3 of *The Writings of Anna Freud* (N. Y., 1973), 641-49; Marjorie R. Leonard, "Fathers and Daughters: The Significance of 'Fathering' in the Psychosexual Development of the Girl," *International Journal of Psycho-Analysis* 47 (parts 2/3, 1966): 333; Herman Nunberg,

Principles of Psychoanalysis: Their Application to the Neuroses, trans. Madlyn Kahr and Sidney Kahr (N. Y., 1955), 70-71. Paul L. Adams, Judith R. Milner, and Nancy A. Schrepf question whether all father fantasies are Oedipal related. *Fatherless Children* (N. Y., 1984), 327.

"Crisis of Color '66," *Newsweek Magazine* 68 (August 22, 1966): 26; Hazel Erskine, "The Polls: Interracial Socializing," *Public Opinion Quarterly* 37 (Summer 1973): 288-89; Joan Downs, "Black/White Dating," *Life Magazine* 70 (May 28, 1971): 56, 62-66 (italics in original). For another article contemporary with the *Life* survey, see Fletcher Knebel, "Identity...The Black Woman's Burden," *Look Magazine* 33 (September 23, 1969): 77-79. The *Newsweek* poll focused in on "How White Views of the Negro Have Changed," so the data presented in terms of "All Whites" would appear to be acceptable with white women and white men combined. The *Life* poll, however, dealt with "public attitudes toward interracial dating and interracial marriage," but only published data for the total sample of whites and blacks together and for blacks separately. By not also including the data for whites separately, the figures presented are of limited value. Moreover, by combining black women and black men together in the black sample, even some of these data have problems because it was well known that at the time of the survey, more black women than black men were against interracial dating (as the *Life* article itself discussed on pp. 62-63). Likewise, the total sample of four combined groups necessarily fails to present any idea as to the views of white women, black women, white men, and black men as different components of society.

Robert C. Sorensen, *Adolescent Sexuality in Contemporary America* (N. Y., 1973), 104-5, 117, 380-81, 383, 466, TABLES 15, 22, 32. Susan Chace, "The Seventeen Survey: My Generation," *Seventeen Magazine* 48 (October 1989): 99-106. Janet Bode, *Different Worlds: Interracial and Cross-Cultural Dating* (N. Y., 1989), 12.

Charles V. Willie and Joan D. Levy, "Black Is Lonely," *Psychology Today* 5 (March 1972): 50-52; Philip A. Belcastro, "Sexual Behavior Differences Between Black and White Students," *Journal of Sex Research* 21 (February 1985): 56, 63. Along these lines, several other small-scale studies which may be of interest include Larry D. Barnett, "Attitudes Toward Interracial Dating," *Family Life Coor-*

dinator 12 (July-October 1963): 88-92; "Black & White Dating," *Time Magazine* 92 (July 19, 1968): 48-49; Hans Sebald, "Patterns of Interracial Dating and Sexual Liaison of White and Black College Men," *International Journal of Sociology of the Family* 4 (Spring 1974): 23-36. Regarding the merits of small-scale studies, see Edward M. Brecher with Jeremy Brecher, "Extracting Valid Sexological Findings from Severely Flawed and Biased Population Samples," *Journal of Sex Research* 22 (February 1986): 8.

"Crisis," *Newsweek,* 26; Erskine, "The Polls," 290, 292. For the general remarks of Frank A. Petroni, see "Teen-Age Interracial Dating," *Trans-Action* 8 (September 1971): 54-59 and his "Interracial Dating - The Price is High," in *Interracial Marriage: Expectations and Realities,* ed. Irving R. Stuart and Lawrence E. Abt (N. Y., 1973), chap. 8.

George H. Gallup, *The Gallup Poll: Public Opinion 1972-1977* (Wilmington, 1978), 1:72, *The Gallup Poll: Public Opinion 1978,* 218, and *The Gallup Poll: Public Opinion 1983,* 96. Regarding the data from the "Virginia Slims American Women's Opinion Poll," see Alex Bontemps, "National Poll Reveals Startling New Attitudes on Interracial Marriage," *Ebony* 30 (September 1975): 151. For more on public opinion polls dealing with interracial sexual relations, see Erskine, "The Polls," 290-94; Robert J. Sickels, *Race, Marriage, and the Law* (Albuquerque, 1972), 42-43, 116-21; Tom W. Smith and Glenn R. Dempsey, "The Polls: Ethnic Social Distance and Prejudice," *Public Opinion Quarterly* 47 (Winter 1983): 589, 591. Of course, in public opinion surveys regarding social issues such as interracial dating or interracial marriage, it may be argued that composite pictures can be presented by combining data for various groups. True enough, but that point of view still does not negate the fact that black (or nonwhite) perspectives will often be inaccurately perceived. In cases where no significant differences exist in data for various groups, at least a statement to that effect would help readers to evaluate the combined data given.

U. S. Bureau of the Census, *Census of Population: 1960, MARITAL STATUS, Final Report PC(2)-4E,* 160; *Census of Population: 1970, MARITAL STATUS, Final Report PC(2)-4C,* 262; *Census of Population: 1980, MARITAL CHARACTERIS-TICS, Final Report PC80-2-4C,* 175; *Current Population Reports, Series P-20, No. 437, HOUSEHOLD AND FAMILY CHARAC-*

TERISTICS: MARCH 1988, 94. The decennial census of 1980 showed 93,660 marriages between white women and black men and 27,329 marriages between white men and black women, yet for the same year TABLE 55 of the *Statistical Abstracts of the United States: 1989* reported 122,000 and 45,000 respectively, based on the Current Population Survey. Why these discrepancies? A personal communication from the Bureau of the Census (August 24, 1989) to this author provided the explanation. The 1980 decennial census sample was based on approximately 17 million households whereas the Current Population Survey is an annual sample based on approximately 65,000 households. Keeping in mind the two sample sizes and differences in collection and processing procedures, the interracial marriage statistics are reasonably proportionate to the number of all married couples in each survey.

Regarding the rise in marriages between white men and black women, see Laura B. Randolph, "Black Women/White Men, What's Goin' On?" *Ebony* 44 (March 1989): 154+.

Marie Ferguson Peters, "The Black Family - Perpetuating the Myths: An Analysis of Family Sociology Textbook Treatment of Black Families," *Family Coordinator* 23 (October 1974): 350-51; Kris Jeter, "Analytic Essay: Intercultural and Interracial Marriage," *Marriage and Family Review* 5 (Spring 1982): 111; Ernest Porterfield, "Black-American Intermarriage in the United States," *Marriage and Family Review* 5 (Spring 1982): 22. For more on the motive of love, see Hugo G. Beigel, "Problems and Motives in Interracial Relationships," *Journal of Sex Research* 2 (November 1966): 195, and Charles E. Smith, "Negro-White Intermarriage: Forbidden Sexual Union," *Journal of Sex Research* 2 (November 1966): 176. Theoretical considerations are discussed in Bernard I. Murstein, "A Theory of Marital Choice Applied to Interracial Marriage," in *Interracial Marriage: Expectations and Realities,* ed. Irving R. Stuart and Lawrence E. Abt (N. Y., 1973), chap. 2. George C. Homans, *The Human Group* (N. Y., 1950), chap. 5, quote on 111 (italics in original); John Money and Anke A. Ehrhardt, *Man & Woman, Boy & Girl* (Baltimore, 1972), 127.

9

ARE WE LIVING OUT A LEGACY FROM THE PAST?

In the national probability sample of white women, 43% agreed with the belief that the lack of acceptance of interracial sexual relations is at the root of racial prejudice in America today (Belief Statement 9). The ties between sexual relations and racial prejudice can be viewed from many different perspectives. This commentary will look at the past in an attempt to comprehend what its effect has been on the present, keeping in mind that the current status of sex between the races in America is really the product of a long and involved process of social coexistence between whites and blacks. Interracial sexual relations have been a factor in the racial prejudice of the past, and this same factor continues to make its influence felt in the racial prejudice which currently exists.

In Chapter 4 it was demonstrated that from 1662 onward, legislation was established which allowed white men sexual access to black women because subsequent interracial children would follow the status of their mothers. Chapter 5 illustrated how this interracial sex accelerated during slavery days and produced several hundred thousand mulattoes. If biological repugnance truly existed between the races, there would have been no interracial sex and no legislation against interracial marriage. However, there was and is sex between the races, so the issue is to explain the psychological repugnance which has been and continues to be expressed toward interracial sexual relations in general. A perspective taken from the pages of history may provide one explanation, and that is, the threat which attractive and intelligent mulattoes posed to the system of slavery and the response of racial theorists, particularly Josiah Clark Nott, who sought to poison public opinion against their freedom. Nott and his followers lived back then and are long dead and gone; however, as the title of this chapter suggests, we may well be living out their legacy without even being aware of it.

To begin with, from the late 1700s onward many observations

were made about mulattoes being very physically attractive. Thomas Anburey, a British Revolutionary War lieutenant, remarked upon visiting a plantation in Virginia,

> There were mulattoes of all tinges, from the first remove, to one almost white; there were some of them young women, who were really beautiful, being extremely well made, and with pretty delicate features.

In 1835, reflecting on those Americans who viewed the mulatto negatively, English traveler Edward S. Abdy recalled

> the dread they entertain that the species will be deteriorated by "crossing the breed"; though every one knows, who is capable of comparing forms and figures, that the finest specimens of beauty and symmetry are to be found among those whose veins are filled with mixed blood.

Some mulattoes particularly those who were light-complexioned (the so-called quadroons and octoroons) were able to advance themselves in the concubinage system of New Orleans, Charleston, and Mobile. Laws prohibited intermarriage, but somewhat permanent relationships were established between intelligent and attractive free mulatto women and nonslaveholding men. Anyone thinking the mulatto inferior or incapable of betterment had only to observe such women, as Frederick L. Olmsted did:

> I refer to a class composed of the illegitimate offspring of white men and coloured women (mulattoes or quadroons)....They are generally pretty, often handsome. I have rarely, if ever, met more beautiful women than one or two whom I saw by chance, in the streets. They are better formed, and have a more graceful and elegant carriage than Americans in general.

Not only were these women beautiful, they were intelligent as well. Many spoke both French and English, and some even spoke French, English, *and* Spanish. Contrary to much of the popular thinking of the time, the intelligence of such mulattoes was not limited to their white parentage. In 1806 anthropologist Johann Friedrich Blumenbach noted "remarkable examples of the perfectibility of the mental faculties and the talents of the Negro." He described intellectual and genius-level blacks in the fields of mathematical and physical sciences, medicine, craftsmanship, music, and the literary arts. Johann David Schoepf, a German physician and naturalist who traveled throughout the Southern states in 1783 and 1784, referred to an earlier remark by Blumenbach regarding the intelligence of blacks and added, "An impartial, unprejudiced observer might assemble among the American Negro slaves, notwithstanding their unfavorable situation, numerous instances in support of this undeniable truth." Others in their writings made similar references, but in keeping with the social standards of slavery times, few could dare to admit to the intelligence of blacks, for even to allude to the possibility would be to threaten the very stability of the social system, in slavery and in everyday caste and class as well. An extraordinary exception to this common thinking was a judicial case in Tennessee in 1846 which included these unusually candid remarks: "A slave is not in the condition of a horse...he is made after the image of the Creator. He has mental capacities, and an immortal principle in his nature, that constitute him equal to his owner, but for the accidental position in which fortune has placed him."

In 1811 in a remarkable statement for the time, Dr. Benjamin Rush, a signer of the Declaration of Independence, made the following observation about the mulatto:

> It is possible, the strength of the intellects may
> be improved in their original conformation, as
> much as the strength of the body, by certain
> mixtures of persons of different nations, habits,
> and constitutions, in marriage. The mulatto
> has been remarked, in all countries, to exceed,
> in sagacity, his white and black parent.

Modern historian Robert Brent Toplin has researched the attitudes of whites toward mulattoes in the South during the period from 1830 to 1861. He has concluded that they were often thought of as physically attractive and intelligent and were frequently taught skills and given extraordinary responsibilities. By asserting that blacks were "improved" by the addition of "Caucasian blood," the widespread practice of sex with black women was able to be both justified and rationalized. This view, however, made slavery more difficult to defend because it elicited an unexpected response from the antislavery forces in the North who now had a stronger position by asserting that "mulatto superiority" made many slaves white-like. If the amount of white admixture related to the amount of white attributes, then nearly white mulattoes seemed to be qualifying for emancipation. Keeping such mulattoes enslaved became difficult for the South to defend, yet to emancipate them was unthinkable because to do so would be to undermine the very integrity of the slavery system itself. Moreover, attractive light-complexioned nearly white mulatto women would not be sexually accessible in freedom as they were in slavery. Illicit sexual relationships with free mulattoes could become legitimate marriages, and with marriages would come racial equality and an end to slavery forever.

The South defended the enslavement of *all* mulattoes as well as legal prohibitions against interracial marriage with theories that attacked the idea that mulattoes were approaching conformity with whites, theories promulgated by the well-known physician and surgeon, Dr. Josiah Clark Nott of Mobile, Alabama. Due to the fact that these theories dealt with interracial marriage and had such profound ramifications on the reasoning of the South and ultimately on the thinking of much of the nation, they are worth going into in some detail.

An account of Dr. Nott's ideas begins with the census of 1840, a census in which free blacks and free mulattoes were counted together as the "Free Colored,"* and enslaved blacks and enslaved mulattoes were the aggregate "Slaves." (From here on in these terms will appear in quotation marks when referring to the census.) Nott read about an interpretation of the mortality statistics in this census which showed that there were twice as many deaths for the free group than for the enslaved. Inasmuch as there were a great many free mulattoes among the "Free Colored," he developed a mulatto frailty theory to explain the reasons this group appeared

---

* Free Colored was the term used by the United States census from 1820 through 1860 to denote free blacks and free mulattoes enumerated together.

to be dying at a much faster rate than the "Slaves." He also developed a mulatto sterility theory to explain his "observation" that mulattoes were less prolific than either whites or blacks. These theories were first published in 1843 in an article for the *American Journal of the Medical Sciences* entitled, "The Mulatto a Hybrid — probable extermination of the two races if the Whites and Blacks are allowed to intermarry." Dr. Nott may have been knowledgeable in the field of medicine, but he was certainly no ethnologist. Ridiculous as it seems today, Nott conceived of the mulatto as a hybrid different than either white or black. He reasoned that just as the horse and the donkey are different species and produce a sterile mule as hybrid offspring, so too white and black are different species and produce a sterile mulatto. Of course, mulattoes produced children like everyone else, so the sterility theory incorporated the idea that fertility deteriorated through subsequent generations with sterility being the inevitable end. Nott conceived of mulattoes as having weak and frail constitutions, high mortality, and infertility. The point of his article was that by keeping slavery legal and interracial marriage illegal, whites and blacks would both remain in existence (presumably because white women who might otherwise marry free black men would marry white men and continue to have white children).

For Dr. Nott whites and blacks did not have a common origin. This theory of inequality refuted the Biblical interpretation of unified humanity and offered support to Southern clergymen who preached the sanctification of slavery from their pulpits. When Nott read the theory of evolution developed by Charles Darwin in his *On the Origin of Species by Means of Natural Selection* (1859), he said of Darwin "the man is Clearly crazy." The idea of whites and blacks being separate species was immediately picked up by other proslavery theorists in support of Dr. Nott. Just to illustrate the absurdity of this whole notion, Dr. Samuel A. Cartwright of New Orleans reasoned that because blacks were a different species than whites they contracted particular mental diseases, and he identified one as Drapetomania, "the disease causing Negroes to run away." We laugh today, but in slavery days such professional assertions were serious business. So serious, in fact, that Cartwright's article was published in 1851 by the famous magazinist James D. B. DeBow in his prestigious *Southern and Western*

Review. DeBow was a notable man in his own right. Besides being a renowned magazinist, he was appointed United States census superintendent in 1853.

Dr. Nott expounded on his concepts of "mulatto inferiority" during the 1840s and 1850s and set the precedence for the "scientific" pronouncements of others. His theories spawned a whole school of followers who were either proslavery or against interracial marriage, and all of their statements of fact were ones of propaganda rather than proof. The "mulatto inferiority" theories of this school seemed to revolve around a theme and variations method. One version, for example, suggested that "the mulatto deteriorates physically in proportion as he ascends in the intellectual scale," a view which shared Nott's original concept whereby the more white admixture mulattoes had, the more vulnerable to physical inferiority they were.

It is easy to see the reason the South seized hold of these views and embraced them. Keeping mulattoes enslaved would keep them legally apart from whites. By conceiving of mulattoes as being of a physically different type, even intelligent light-complexioned mulattoes were still considered hybrids and not nearly white as the antislavery North had claimed. The continued enslavement of all mulattoes (as well as all blacks) was vindicated and the legal prohibition against interracial marriage was justified.

What is surprising about all of this is that obviously, as indicated by the Virginia law of 1662 and the Maryland law of 1664, there were many mulattoes in America from very early on, and any particular pattern of inferiority certainly would have been observed and commented on long before the 1840s. Just as surprising is the fact that no one seized upon the real explanations in aggregate for the statistical differences between the "Free Colored" and "Slaves" in the 1840 (as well as 1850 and 1860) census figures, and those were *the "passing" of nearly white free mulattoes over into white society as whites, the wholesale illegal importation of new slaves,* and *the wrongful enslavement of free blacks and free mulattoes.* As will become clear, if one is to understand Dr. Nott and his position against interracial marriage, one must have insight into how "passing," slave smuggling, and kidnapping distorted the census statistics on which he based his theories and how these factors *made it appear* that the "Free Colored" population (many of whom were mulattoes) were not as long-lived or as reproductive as the "Slaves."

It is to be pointed out that people are often reluctant to explain things in terms of the immoral side of human nature, and American history is no exception. Smuggling and kidnapping (of adults as well as children) are repulsive ideas. However, as will become evident, the motivation of money and the opportunities to make it explain why Dr. Nott's theories were able to be devised and maintained.

The discussion about the decrease in the census figures for the "Free Colored" population begins with the observation that many light-complexioned nearly white mulattoes "passed" over into white society and lived as whites. Understandably, no figures or even estimates are available due to the totally clandestine and personal nature of such activity, particularly during slavery days. Although "passing" was discussed with regard to runaway slaves who had light complexions, it was not a topic of conversation otherwise. In a rare instance, in 1854 the phenomenon was mentioned by James D. B. DeBow who was census superintendent at the time.

A second way in which the size of the "Free Colored" population was distorted was by the addition of illegally imported slaves to the "Slave" population. Inasmuch as such additions enlarged the total number of "Slaves," when the census figures for the two groups were compared, the increases for the "Free Colored" appeared proportionately smaller. As will be seen, slave smuggling spanned five decades.

On March 2, 1807, congressional legislation was passed which legally prohibited the importation of slaves into the United States as of January 1, 1808. Penalties included the confiscation of slave ships, and fines and imprisonments of up to $20,000 and ten years. The acquisition of the Louisiana Territory, the settlement of the Mississippi Valley, and the annexation of Texas, however, all created intense demands for new slave labor. Moreover, with a rise in the price of cotton and expectations of slavery expansion westward, slave prices began to rise steadily from about 1845 up through and including 1860. From 1808 to 1860 the only sources of new slaves were the progeny from the internal slave trade and smuggling from Africa and Cuba (then an agrarian colony of Spain). As early as 1810 President James Madison reported to Congress that American citizens were defying the newly passed law by illegally trafficking in enslaved Africans. Between 1815 and 1820 over 10,000 slaves *per year* were being smuggled into America. Estimates for 1818 and 1819 each range between 13,000 and 15,000. The scope and magnitude of this smuggling becomes clear when viewed in light of the congressional legislation of March 3, 1819, which granted a $50 bounty to informers for every illegally imported slave seized by officials, and the congressional legislation of May 15, 1820, in which the external slave trade was decreed to be piracy punishable by the death penalty! *All of this legislation was difficult to implement because of unclear enforcement authority on both the federal and state levels, and illicit acquisitions continued on virtually unabated.* In the public forum up to the Civil War, the South demonstrated a strong desire to have the African slave trade legally reopened. This was the major topic addressed at the Southern Commercial Convention at Vicksburg in 1859. For the most part, however, this public posturing was aimed at legalizing and expanding an already existing illicit African slave trade. This illegal activity must have been considered tolerable because many of the slave smugglers who were caught went unpunished and there was no hue and cry of public outrage. Senator Stephen A. Douglas was reported to have said that "the slave-trade had been carried on quite extensively for a long time back" and that 15,000 Africans were illegally imported in 1859 alone, more than during any one year when importations were legal. Douglas never disavowed the statements. During the 1850s slave smuggling became particularly blatant, so much so that even the political party platform on which Lincoln ran in 1860 included a plank about abolishing the illegal African slave trade. The Lincoln government proved true to its word by hanging the first American slave smuggler in 1862.

Even the United States census of 1860 adds an interesting perspective to all of this. The census refers to the population of the slaves and observes,

> The rate of progress of this class of population
> has been somewhat more fluctuating than can
> be easily accounted for. Why, for example, they
> should have increased over 30 per cent. from

> 1820 to 1830, and only 23.8 per cent. during the
> next decade, does not appear from any facts
> bearing upon their condition during this peri-
> od. There is no importation nor emigration of
> slaves into or from the country; and it would
> seem that they should be subject to no cause of
> increase or decadence except what nature
> decrees.

This statement, of course, does not acknowledge even the possibility that illegally imported slaves influenced the statistics, despite a
later reference in the text to "Africans captured on several slave
ships," an allusion to unsuccessful attempts at slave smuggling.
Even in the absence of an official statement regarding illegal
importation, it is incontrovertible that thousands upon thousands of slaves were unlawfully brought into the United States and
added to the slave populations of the South. Back in 1839 just one
year prior to the census of 1840 from which Dr. Nott based his
early work, the antislavery pamphlet *American Slavery as It Is*
correctly pointed out that many thousands of illegally imported
Africans were being added to the slave numbers in each census. In
1850 even Nott himself acknowledged that the slave population
was doubling every thirty years, an intriguing observation in light
of the high degree of mortality among slaves. Although the actual
number of slaves who were illicitly brought into America from
Cuba and Africa can never be known due to the clandestine and
indeterminate nature of smuggling, realistic estimates have placed
the figure at about a quarter of a million.

A third way in which the census statistics for the "Free Colored"
population were distorted compared with those for the "Slaves"
had to do with the wrongful enslavement of free blacks and free
mulattoes who were kidnapped and sold back into slavery. Not
only did this practice decrease the "Free Colored" population, it
simultaneously increased the "Slave" population. In 1839 the
antislavery pamphlet *American Slavery as It Is* stated that "in all
probability, *each* United States' census of the *slave* population, is
increased by the addition to it of *thousands* of free colored persons,
kidnapped and sold as slaves."

Such kidnappings were made all the more conducive after
congressional passage of the controversial Fugitive Slave Act of

1850 which virtually condoned such activity because it denied *all* blacks and mulattoes legal protection, runaway slaves as well as those who were legitimately free. With the civil rights of all blacks and mulattoes suspended, slaveholders or anyone else could *claim* a free black or free mulatto to be their runaway slave and there was little that could be done about it (PLATE 8). In this manner along with outright kidnapping, many free blacks and free mulattoes were sold back into slavery with their abductors having virtual impunity. Samuel May, Jr., a minister involved in the movement to abolish slavery, reflected on the fugitive slave law and in 1861 wrote that it "was well called, by the New York *Evening Post,* 'An Act for the Encouragement of Kidnapping'."

Kidnapping was widespread and was not limited to free blacks and free mulattoes. Many people who belonged to the antislavery movement as well as those sympathetic to its cause were rightly concerned that if nearly white free mulattoes could be enslaved, then white people themselves could be also (PLATES 9, 10). *It is important to understand that whether or not you were a slave was not determined by your color.* The fundamental principle on which American slavery was built was that the child follows the status of the mother (see Chapter 4). If a nearly white mulatto slave mother who herself might easily pass as being white had a virtually white child, her child was also a slave...period. Those who feared the encroachment of slavery into white society had their view affirmed in accounts such as that of George William Featherstonhaugh, an Englishman who traveled throughout the South during 1834 and 1835. In New Orleans he observed,

> A woman may be as fair as any European, and have no symptom of Negro blood about her; she may have received a virtuous education, have been brought up with the greatest tenderness, may possess various accomplishments, and may be eminently calculated to act the part of a faithful wife and tender mother; but if it can be proved that she has *one drop of Negro blood* in her veins, the laws do not permit her to contract a marriage with a white man.

Concern over white people being kidnapped and sold into slavery peaked in the 1850s just when slave prices were rising rapidly. Such concern was exemplified, for example, in the many references to white slavery in *The Suppressed Book about Slavery! Prepared for Publication in 1857, - Never Published Until the Present Time* (New York, 1864), attributed to the New York bookdealer and printer, George Washington Carleton. Certainly, the number of white people who were kidnapped and sold into slavery must have been relatively few compared to the scale on which such activity was conducted with free blacks and free mulattoes. The point to bear in mind, however, is that *the potential for such white kidnapping was ever present.*

In light of the poor financial position of many individuals and families in the antebellum South, those whites who could be motivated by illicit money had strong inducement to become involved in either illegal importations or domestic abductions. Historian William E. Dodd has estimated that around 1850, hundreds of thousands of families in the cotton states were each receiving a monetary return averaging less than $100 a year. The plantation gentry aside, many people throughout much of the South had little money. Those with low income included the so-called "poor whites" and yeoman farmers with little or no cash crop who lived at subsistence level. Of course, in terms of the national picture, poor Southerners were far from the only ones who had reason to be attracted to the illegal slave trade. In 1860 the daily wages paid to a day laborer in the aggregate of all states and territories averaged $1.18, so working six days a week could earn upward of $300 a year which was a decent living in those days. Putting the monetary value of slaves into perspective, in 1860 the price of a prime male field hand was $1,800 in New Orleans and Georgia, $1,200 in Virginia, and about $1,250 in Charleston. Remarkable but true, it may be said that when slave prices were at their highest, one prime male slave had a cash value comparable to what a day laborer might earn in three to four years. Certainly, carpenters and others in the skilled trades earned higher wages, lesser quality slaves brought lower prices, and all slave prices were lower prior to 1860. Even with these factors taken into consideration, it is easy to see just how profitable slave smuggling and kidnapping really were.

Consider the scope of illegal importations for a moment. In 1857

CAUTION!!

COLORED PEOPLE
OF BOSTON, ONE & ALL,

You are hereby respectfully CAUTIONED and advised, to avoid conversing with the

Watchmen and Police Officers of Boston,

For since the recent ORDER OF THE MAYOR & ALDERMEN, they are empowered to act as

KIDNAPPERS
AND
Slave Catchers,

And they have already been actually employed in KIDNAPPING, CATCHING, AND KEEPING SLAVES. Therefore, if you value your LIBERTY, and the *Welfare of the Fugitives* among you, *Shun* them in every possible manner, as so many *HOUNDS* on the track of the most unfortunate of your race.

Keep a Sharp Look Out for KIDNAPPERS, and have TOP EYE open.

APRIL 24, 1851.

PLATE 8

MASSACHUSETTS PLACARD concerned with the
Fugitive Slave Act of 1850 and the
kidnapping of free blacks and free mulattoes

ANTI-SLAVE-CATCHERS'
MASS
CONVENTION!

All the People of this State, who are opposed to being made SLAVES or SLAVE-CATCHERS, and to having the Free Soil of Wisconsin made the hunting-ground for *Human Kidnappers*, and all who are willing to unite in a

☞ STATE LEAGUE, ☜

to defend our State Sovereignty, our State Courts, and our State and National Constitutions, against the flagrant usurpations of U. S. Judges, Commissioners, and Marshals, and their Attorneys; and to maintain inviolate those great Constitutional Safeguards of Freedom—the WRIT OF HABEAS CORPUS, and the RIGHT OF TRIAL BY JURY—as old and sacred as Constitutional Liberty itself; and all who are willing to sustain the cause of those who are prosecuted, and to be prosecuted in Wisconsin, by the agents and executors of the Kidnapping Act of 1850, for the alleged crime of rescuing a human being from the hands of kidnappers, and restoring him to himself and to Freedom, are invited to meet at

YOUNGS' HALL,
IN THIS CITY,

THURSDAY, APRIL 13th,

At 11 o'clock A. M., to counsel together, and take such action as the exigencies of the times, and the cause of imperilled Liberty demand.

FREEMEN OF WISCONSIN! In the spirit of our Revolutionary Fathers, come up to this gathering of the Free, resolved to speak and act as men worthy of a Free Heritage. Let the plough stand still in the furrow, and the door of the workshop be closed, while you hasten to the rescue of your country. Let the Merchant forsake his Counting Room, the Lawyer his Brief, and the Minister of God his Study, and come up to discuss with us the broad principles of Liberty. Let Old Age throw aside its crutch, and Youth put on the strength of manhood, and the young men gird themselves anew for the conflict; and faith ..., make us valiant in fight, and hope lead us onward to victory; "for they that be for us, are ..., than they that be against us." Come, then, one and all, from every town and village, come, and unite with us in the sacred cause of Liberty. *Now* is the time to strike for Freedom. *Come,* while the *free* spirit still *burns* in your bosom. *Come!* ere the fires of Liberty are extinguished on the nation's altars, and it be too late to re-kindle the dying embers.

BY ORDER OF COMMITTEE OF ARRANGEMENTS.
MILWAUKEE, April 7, 1854.

PLATE 9

WISCONSIN PLACARD (Milwaukee - April 7, 1854)
"opposed to being made SLAVES"
refers to the kidnapping of white people
"the Kidnapping Act of 1850" is a
synonym for the Fugitive Slave Act of 1850

REPUBLICAN BULLETIN, No. 9.

THE ISSUE.

WHITE SLAVERY.

THE EXTENSION OF SLAVERY IS THE QUESTION NOT ONLY OVER **FREE SOIL**, BUT OVER **FREE MEN**. DO YOU DOUBT IT? READ THE WORDS OF THE HIGHEST AUTHORITIES IN THE SOUTH.

The *Richmond (Va.) Enquirer*, the oldest Democratic paper in the Old Dominion, a most able supporter of Buchanan for the Presidency, and of the Cincinnati Platform, speaks thus on this question. We take its own forcible words.

"Until recently, the defence of Slavery has labored under great difficulties, because its apologists, (for they were mere apologists,) took half way ground. They confined the defence of slavery to mere negro slavery; thereby giving up the slavery *principle*, admitting *other* forms of slavery to be *wrong*.

"The line of defence, however, is now changed. The South maintains that SLAVERY IS RIGHT, NATURAL AND NECESSARY, AND DOES NOT DEPEND UPON DIFFERENCE OF COMPLEXION. THE LAWS OF THE SLAVE STATES JUSTIFY THE HOLDING OF WHITE MEN IN BONDAGE."

Another leading press of the Democratic party, and a worthy organ of Mr. Buchanan, published in South Carolina, sustains the views we have quoted from the Enquirer. It uses this plain, straightforward language on the subject :—

"*Slavery is the natural and normal condition of the laboring man, whether white or black.* The great evil of Northern *free* society is, that it is burthened with a SERVILE CLASS OF MECHANICS AND LABORERS, UNFIT FOR SELF-GOVERNMENT, and yet clothed with the attributes and powers of citizens. Master and slave is a relation in society as necessary as that of parent and child; and the Northern States will yet have to introduce it. Their *theory of a free government is a delusion.*"

But there is still broader ground on the subject of society, taken by the *Richmond Enquirer*. It says, in a recent number :—

"Repeatedly have we asked the North, 'Has not the experiment of universal liberty FAILED? Are not the evils of FREE SOCIETY INSUFFERABLE? And do not most thinking men among you propose to subvert and reconstruct it?' Still no answer. This gloomy silence is another conclusive proof, added to many other conclusive evidences we have furnished, THAT FREE SOCIETY, IN THE LONG RUN, IS AN IMPRACTICABLE FORM OF SOCIETY."

Another paper, published in Virginia, the *South Side Democrat*, a journal distinguished for its faithful support of Mr. Buchanan, says :

"We have got to hating everything with the prefix FREE, from free negroes down and up through the whole catalogue—FREE farms, FREE labor, FREE society, FREE will, FREE thinking, FREE children, and FREE schools—all belonging to the same brood of *damnable isms*. But the worst of all these abominations, is the modern system of FREE SCHOOLS."

PLATE 10

Portion of REPUBLICAN PARTY HANDBILL
from the election of 1856

an American missionary in West Africa reported that the price for an able-bodied male slave there was just $40. Compare this to the thousand dollar figures just cited. Immense profits were being made in illegal importations even before the huge run-up of slave prices that occurred between 1845 and 1860. In the late 1820s slaves could be obtained for as little as $18 to $20. In 1827 a smuggling outfit paid the high price of $50 each for one cargo of 217 slaves, sold them at an average of $357 each, and realized the outrageous profit of over $40,000 (a small fortune in terms of 1820s dollars). In the late 1830s a slave purchased for $20 to $30 in Africa would bring between $250 and $350 in Cuba and several times that amount in American slave markets. Expenses notwithstanding, profits were enormous. Smuggling slaves from Cuba into the Southern states was extremely lucrative as well. For example, in 1851 a slave valued at $300 to $400 in Cuba would bring $800 to $1,000 in Louisiana. In 1854 the price spread was $500 in Cuba and $1,200 in Louisiana. These monetary figures take on profound meaning considering that the daily wages paid to a day laborer in the states and territories averaged $1.11 in 1850. This state of affairs was by no means limited to the latter antebellum period. Even back in the late 1830s when such wages were less than $1.00, David Turnbull, an English traveler, visited Cuba and reported:

> When I was at the Havana, the average price of Bozal [newly imported] Negroes, when purchased at wholesale by the cargo, was at the rate of from 300 to 320 dollars a head, whereas I have had the misfortune to witness the sale of slaves by auction, when three times the price has been offered in the public streets of Richmond, Virginia, and elsewhere in that section of the Union.

In a reference to Texas, Turnbull wrote of "the well-known fact, that the price of a slave at Houston or Galveston is three or four times as great as it ever is at the Havana."

In addition to illicit importations, the domestic abductions described earlier were the second illegal source of new slaves and huge profits. In 1839 the antislavery writer William Jay remarked, "An able-bodied colored man sells in the Southern market for from eight hundred to a thousand dollars; of course he is worth

stealing....it is not strange it should be extensively practised."
In 1853 Harriet Beecher Stowe spoke of free blacks and free
mulattoes and noted, "Around the [slave] trader are continually
passing and repassing men and women who would be worth to him
thousands of dollars in the way of trade – who belong to a class
whose rights nobody respects, and who, if reduced to slavery, could
not easily make their word good against him. The probability is
that hundreds of free men and women and children are all the time
being precipitated into slavery in this way."

Whether illicit importation or domestic kidnapping, there were
incalculable amounts of money to be made by everyone involved in
the illegal slave trade. *All of this unlawful activity could not help but
influence the census numbers.* When the population increases for
"Free Colored" and "Slaves" are compared in the census data for
1800 through 1860, the "Free Colored" show less increases for
1820, 1840, 1850 and 1860, and it was during these very times
that slave prices for the most part were accelerating upward. Even
with the financial Panic of 1857 when cotton prices took a downturn
and continued in that direction, slave prices not only kept on
climbing higher but reached all-time highs!

Dr. Nott's theories justified the continued enslavement of *all*
mulattoes as well as blacks. In order to understand the impact
which these "mulatto inferiority" theories had on the thinking of
pre-Civil War America, it is necessary to understand something
about the proslavery politics of those days because the South had a
great deal to gain *politically* by retaining the institution of slavery
and constantly expanding it. The three-fifths compromise incorporated into the United States Constitution apportioned representation in the House of Representatives and in the electoral college
by counting five slaves as three free persons. In addition to the
pecuniary gains from slavery which in and of themselves were
substantial, large numbers of slaves gave the South political representation in Congress with a strong proslavery vote and power
to greatly influence national policy. It is a well-known fact, for
example, that the election of Thomas Jefferson was swayed in this
manner. In the words of historians Nathaniel Weyl and William
Marina, "The compromise gave the South, in every election between

1790 and the Civil War, from a quarter to a third more Representatives in Congress than her free population entitled her to have." It may be said that much of the time the South virtually controlled Congress. In 1857 statisticians Henry Chase and C. H. Sanborn observed, "It will be seen that in the late severe contests in the House of Representatives, had freemen only been represented, the question would invariably have been decided in favor of the North." Obviously, the Southern states and slavery were politically inseparable. Such political power became commonly known as the "Slave Power."

In order to defend slavery against its opponents, propaganda techniques were brought into play. The mulatto/hybrid issue which Dr. Nott raised in 1843 was not the first. Two years earlier the 1840 census was published which listed *falsified figures* for insanity among free blacks and free mulattoes in the North. The idea was to show the North *proof* that the slaves could not survive on their own because they would degenerate mentally if they were freed. These 1840 census figures were scandalous. Even proslavery Southerner James D. B. DeBow, destined to become census superintendent himself in 1853, had to concede, "The number of insane Negroes was marked, we believe, higher in one state than the whole amount of Negroes registered in it." John C. Calhoun, senator from South Carolina who became secretary of state in 1844, spoke in detail of the census statistics for the "Free Colored" and declared that it would be disastrous for the country and for the blacks themselves if the slaves were freed. John Quincy Adams attempted several times to conduct an inquiry into the census of 1840 but Southern congressional power resisted. In his *Memoirs,* Adams recalled a meeting he had with Calhoun:

> He writhed like a trodden rattlesnake on the exposure of his false report to the House that no material errors have been discovered in the printed census of 1840, and finally said that where there were so many errors they balanced one another, and led to the same conclusion as if they were all correct.

Harriet Beecher Stowe related that it was popular to cite the census of 1840 in discussions about mulatto inferiority. She declared,

> *The false returns stand to this day in the
> statistical tables of the census,* to convince all
> cavillers of the unfitness of the Negro for
> freedom....*In order to gain capital for the
> extension of slave territory, the most impor-
> tant statistical document of the United States
> has been boldly, grossly, and perseveringly
> falsified, and stands falsified to this day.*
> Query: If State documents are falsified in sup-
> port of slavery, what confidence can be placed
> in *any* representations that are made upon the
> subject?

Medical historian Albert Deutsch has looked at the census of
1840 as proslavery propaganda and really put the damage done
into its fullest perspective when he wrote, "The flagrant, socially
harmful errors of the 1840 census continued to be spread abroad
under the sanction of Congress. The errors repeatedly found their
way into lay and professional journals." Dr. Nott's "mulatto
inferiority" theories which first appeared in 1843 were given
support by the 1840 census figures for insanity among free blacks
and free mulattoes. The propaganda picture was now complete.
Nott's theories regarding the *physical degeneration* of frailty
and sterility did not exist in isolation, but rather, coexisted with
the notions that enslaved blacks and enslaved mulattoes in the
South were mentally competent but free blacks and free mulattoes
in the North were prone to *mental degeneration* and unfit for
their freedom.

In the end, "mulatto inferiority" had absolutely nothing whatsoever to do with the true reasons why the increase for the "Free
Colored" population was less than that for the "Slaves" in the
1840 census figures which Dr. Nott studied. Free blacks and free
mulattoes lived, died, and had children just as the slaves did. The
decrease in the "Free Colored" group reflected "passing" and
wrongfully enslaved free blacks and free mulattoes, while their
increase was limited to children and a number of manumitted
slaves. On the other hand, the increase in the "Slave" group
consisted of children, free blacks and free mulattoes who were
wrongfully enslaved, and large numbers of newly smuggled slaves.
Moreover, many of these newly smuggled slaves were prime adults

of childbearing years, so their early offspring added to the numbers, thereby compounding the increase further. Nott's theories about mulattoes with their physical frailty, high mortality, and sterility became powerful arguments in dealing with Northern antislavery forces who considered light-complexioned nearly white mulattoes as qualifying for freedom. In his view, such freedom would inevitably result in these "frail and sterile" mulattoes intermarrying with whites, and that would be the beginning of the end for slavery, if not humanity itself. Southern propaganda and the census of 1840 completed the picture by adding the factor of mental degeneration as well.

The "mulatto inferiority" theories which Dr. Nott and his followers circulated during the 1840s and 1850s permeated society and became widely accepted public opinion. One notable exception to this general rule of acceptance appeared in 1855. Southern educator and statistician George Tucker examined the 1850 census and concluded, "Some physiologists are disposed to regard mulattoes as hybrids, and as exhibiting in their greater shortness of life, the degeneracy of that class; but a comparative table of the blacks and mulattoes in two States – Connecticut and Louisiana, and two cities – New York and New Orleans, disproves this hypothesis." Few agreed with Tucker's point of view, for by 1855 Nott's theories had become engrained in the popular imagination. That these ideas were so generally widespread is all the more understandable in light of the high degree of illiteracy among whites in the antebellum South and their being very impressionable. Even Frederick L. Olmsted, an intelligent and educated Northern journalist who traveled throughout the South, acknowledged the popularity of these theories but predictably disagreed with them. In his writings about New Orleans, he stated that

> the French quadroons are very handsome and healthy in appearance; and I should not be surprised if really thorough and sufficient scientific observation should show them to be – contrary to the common assertion – more vigorous than either of the parent races.

He also reported that the Southerners with whom he spoke did not support any of the views about mulatto inferiority. Had Olmsted asked others, however, their response might have been different. Take John S. Wilson, an M. D. from Georgia, for example. An article he wrote for the agricultural journal *American Cotton Planter and Soil of the South* (1858) stated the following, true to the common understanding of the day:

> While Negroes are generally long-lived, the contrary is true of mulattoes, enjoying the same advantages. This may arise from want of congeniality in the mixture of white and black blood, but, whatever the explanation, there can be but little doubt of the *fact,* for it seems to be established by the concurrent testimony of numerous observers.

The influence of Dr. Nott spread into contemporary popular literature as well. In the *Southern Quarterly Review* (1853), the noted writer Louisa S. McCord used the concept of "mulatto inferiority" in her attack on the light-complexioned, intelligent, and attractive mulatto characters in Harriet Beecher Stowe's *Uncle Tom's Cabin.* Alluding to the issue of sterility, she stated that mulattoes are "incapable of ranking with the white[s]" because they are "not capable of continuous transmission." McCord thought that Stowe was promoting interracial marriage and assailed her by declaring, "All spirit of joking leaves us as we look shudderingly forward to *her* results. Amalgamation is evidently no bugbear to this lady." Newspapers also made pejorative references to the mulatto. An editorial in the *Boston Daily Courier* (September 24, 1860) stated, "We believe the mulatto to be inferior in capacity, character, and organization." The sterility issue was addressed in an editorial in the *New York Journal of Commerce* (October 26, 1860) in which it was said, "Negroes and whites cannot perpetuate a new race."

Historian Joel Williamson has observed that during the 1850s there was a steep increase in the hostility expressed toward the free mulatto. This is quite understandable in light of the fact that the free mulatto represented the greatest interracial sexual threat. The fallacious and loathsome "ethnology" of Dr. Nott and his followers had its desired effect. After all, many mulattoes were intelligent and attractive, but what about their frailty and sterility? Concubinage in slavery was one thing, but how could anyone in good conscience even begin to accept the idea of interracial marriage knowing that children could be of an inferior physical constitution?

What is so utterly amazing about all of this is the extent to which people readily accepted Nott's theories in the complete absence of proof. Reginald Horsman, Dr. Josiah Clark Nott's biographer, has documented how despite many attempts, Nott was never able to prove any of his "mulatto inferiority" theories. Even as late as 1864 Dr. Thomas L. Nichols, an American who lived and published in England, wrote of mulattoes being weak and short-lived after referring to Dr. Nott as "one of the most distinguished of American ethnologists."

Perhaps the one example most indicative of the scope and extent to which Nott's theories spread was the official United States population census for 1860. In those days the census was more than just columns of statistics. The superintendent of the census was at liberty to (objectively) comment and interpret. In this supposedly unbiased and impartial document, Superintendent Joseph C. G. Kennedy wrote:

> As but two censuses have been taken which discriminate between the blacks and mulattoes, it is not yet so easy to determine how far the admixture of the races affects their vital power; but the developments already made would indicate that *the mingling of the races is more unfavorable to vitality, than a condition of slavery,* which practically ignores marriage to the exclusion of the admixture of races, *has proved.*

He went on to say that the population increase for the slaves as a whole was proportionately greater than for its mulatto component, the implication being that the slave mulattoes were not reproducing to the same extent as the slave blacks. In other words, slave mulattoes did not have the same vitality as either whites or slave blacks, and inasmuch as slavery ignored marriage and kept the races mixing illegitimately, the mulattoes with their frailty and sterility problems were confined to the slave population, well away from legitimate intermarriage with whites. What is particularly interesting about this proslavery viewpoint is that it was published in 1864, *after* Lincoln had already freed the slaves in the Confederate states. In another reference, Kennedy again speaks of "mulatto inferiority" by stating:

> The extinction of slavery, in widening the field
> for white labor and enterprise, will tend to re-
> duce the rate of increase of the colored race,
> while its diffusion will lead to a more rapid ad-
> mixture, the tendency of which, judging from
> the past, will be to *impair it physically* without
> improving it morally.

Earlier he spoke of "whatever deterioration may be the consequence of this alloyage."

It appears that these remarks and others Kennedy made in the census cost him his job. *Population* and *Agriculture,* the first two volumes of the 1860 census, had been published in 1864. Kennedy was right in the midst of *Manufactures,* the third volume, when his position as superintendent of the census was terminated on June 7, 1865. Congress, at the time without Southern congressmen because of Secession, did not appropriate the funds necessary to continue Kennedy's position. His duties were transferred to the commissioner of the General Land Office who was charged with completing the third and fourth volumes (PLATE 11). Congressman Addison Henry Laflin stated, "The reason for the transfer was that there was an unappropriated fund under the charge of the Commissioner of the General Land Office which could be as well applied to this purpose as to any other, and it was impossible to continue the publication of the Census Reports without making this transfer." The October 21, 1865 edition of the *Daily Constitutional Union,* a Washington, D. C. newspaper, reported that the first two volumes of the 1860 census were a great success throughout the United States and in Europe and remarked that Kennedy was "suddenly and without cause disconnected with labors to which he is so well adapted." When the widespread achievements of *Population* and *Agriculture* are weighed against the arbitrary quality of Laflin's comments, it seems entirely reasonable to suggest that Kennedy

POPULATION

OF

THE UNITED STATES

IN

1860;

COMPILED FROM THE ORIGINAL RETURNS

OF

THE EIGHTH CENSUS,

UNDER THE

DIRECTION OF THE SECRETARY OF THE INTERIOR,

By JOSEPH C. G. KENNEDY,
SUPERINTENDENT OF CENSUS.

WASHINGTON:
GOVERNMENT PRINTING OFFICE.
1864.

AGRICULTURE

OF

THE UNITED STATES

IN

1860;

COMPILED FROM THE ORIGINAL RETURNS

OF

THE EIGHTH CENSUS,

UNDER THE

DIRECTION OF THE SECRETARY OF THE INTERIOR,

By JOSEPH C. G. KENNEDY,
SUPERINTENDENT OF CENSUS.

WASHINGTON:
GOVERNMENT PRINTING OFFICE.
1864.

MANUFACTURES

OF

THE UNITED STATES

IN

1860;

COMPILED FROM THE ORIGINAL RETURNS

OF

THE EIGHTH CENSUS,

UNDER THE

DIRECTION OF THE SECRETARY OF THE INTERIOR.

WASHINGTON:
GOVERNMENT PRINTING OFFICE.
1865.

STATISTICS

OF

THE UNITED STATES,
(INCLUDING MORTALITY, PROPERTY, &c.,)

IN

1860;

COMPILED FROM THE ORIGINAL RETURNS AND BEING THE FINAL EXHIBIT

OF

THE EIGHTH CENSUS,

UNDER THE

DIRECTION OF THE SECRETARY OF THE INTERIOR.

WASHINGTON:
GOVERNMENT PRINTING OFFICE.
1866.

PLATE 11

UNITED STATES CENSUS OF 1860
the name JOSEPH C. G. KENNEDY
is noticeably absent from volumes three and four

could have been retained if there was a congressional desire to do so. Even the *Daily Constitutional Union* commented, "It seems singular that, for the want of funds sufficient to pay the salary of the Superintendent of the Census, a work which thus far has been so successfully prosecuted should be assigned to the charge of a Bureau with sufficient duties to occupy its attention; and this at a moment when it appears so easy to find the means, with or without law, to organize Bureaus and incur expenditures never contemplated by Congress." The salary issue is all the more curious considering the fact that on March 4, 1864, only a year and three months prior to Kennedy's termination, a committee of the House of Representatives remarked that his salary "is a reasonable one." In light of Kennedy's promulgation of Dr. Nott's "mulatto inferiority" theories in the first volume of the 1860 census, one might speculate that he was removed from his position as census superintendent prior to working on the fourth volume which included statistics about mortality. Dr. Edward Jarvis, a physician and renowned statistician, compiled the mortality statistics for the 1860 census and spoke of mulattoes inheriting from both parents "their powers and their weaknesses, their susceptibilities and their energies." These remarks were in sharp contrast with the pejorative ones made by Kennedy.

It is very unfortunate indeed that Joseph C. G. Kennedy's commentaries have remained as part of the official 1860 census because modern readers who are unfamiliar with the historical context in which they were made will take them to be true and government sanctioned. The odious, widespread, and totally inaccurate beliefs about the mulatto that permeated society up to the highest levels were nothing more than false arguments used to defend the institution of slavery. Even so, as will be seen, they were to continue to have a profound and lasting influence long after slavery was abolished.

Back in the 1850s, however, slavery was still a powerful force and as antislavery pressures continued to build, interracial sexual relations became a hot political issue. Many people, Northerners and Southerners alike, either held or were familiar with the view that the abolition of slavery meant certain amalgamation. There were good reasons for this thinking. Over many years antislavery forces in the

North preached of large-scale interracial sexual relations existing between Southern white men and their black (used from here on in to mean black and mulatto together) concubines, and as mentioned previously even Southern men themselves such as William Harper, James Henry Hammond, and William Gilmore Simms acknowledged the practice. If the slaves were freed and became equal with whites, it was thought that a considerable amount of interracial marriages would take place because of pressures to legitimize many of these existing relationships, and with black migration North, the establishment of many new ones. It may be said that the sight of a mulatto in either the North or the South confirmed the *reality* of interracial sexuality for all to see. Add to this the distorted census statistics and commentaries of 1840, 1850 and 1860 by which Southern propaganda depicted the mulatto as an inferior being, reinforced by warnings about interracial marriage coming from the pens of Dr. Nott and his followers during these years, and there was plenty for people to worry about.

Abraham Lincoln addressed the idea of abolition and certain amalgamation in his speech of June 26, 1857, in which he stated, "Now I protest against the counterfeit logic which concludes that, because I do not want a black woman for a *slave* I must necessarily want her for a *wife*. I need not have her for either, I can just leave her alone." To compound the issue further, many whites mistakenly thought that it was the blacks who wanted to intermarry, however, as the black author and publisher David Ruggles had said back in 1834:

> Abolitionists do not wish "amalgamation." I do not wish it, nor does any colored man or woman of my acquaintance, nor can instances be adduced where a desire was manifested by any colored person; but I deny that "intermarriages" between the "whites and blacks are unnatural"....Let it become fashionable (God grant it never may) for white and colored persons to intermarry and the "repugnance" will vanish like dew before the rising sun.

The notion of interracial sexual relations permeated society to such a degree that even the popular literature of the time dealt with the subject. James Kinney, a professor of English, has compiled a list of twenty-seven novels published between 1835 and 1865 which involve either interracial sex or marriage.

The amalgamation issue reached its peak in late December 1863 in New York City, when an anonymous pamphlet appeared entitled *Miscegenation: The Theory of the Blending of the Races, Applied to the American White Man and Negro* (New York, 1864). Authorship has been attributed to two journalists, David Goodman Croly and George Wakeman. The main thesis of the pamphlet was that the complete blending of the races was the one obvious solution to the race issue. Among other very controversial ideas of the day, it suggested that white women could be sexually attracted to and even fall in love with black men (pp. 42-45). Croly and Wakeman were anti-Lincoln and wrote *Miscegenation* as a political dirty trick. Lincoln had already issued the Emancipation Proclamation and was up for re-election. The intent was to embarrass him and his party by publishing a pamphlet which implied that freeing the slaves promoted interracial sex and marriage.

It was often thought that after the Civil War emancipation would legitimize and encourage interracial sexual relationships, particularly between white women and black men, and for many, the ideas of miscegenation and mulatto inferiority were inseparable. It can be argued that here is where the seed of modern racial prejudice in America took hold. On the one hand, the white man who always had clandestine if not overt sexual access to the black woman without being responsible for the child, now feared that with racial equality, the white woman who endured the interracial double standard would be free to cross the color line herself. On the other hand, in light of Dr. Nott's virulent legacy, it was believed that legal marriages between white women and black men would produce children who were sterile or otherwise physically inferior. Such thinking was maintained through the Civil War and beyond. In light of the implications of mulatto inferiority contained in official government documents, particularly the censuses of 1840 and 1860, as well as an eye toward the readmission of the Southern states and federal reunion, it is no wonder that interracial sexual relations as a state segregation issue played a part in congressional discussions surrounding the Civil Rights Act of 1866 and the Fourteenth Amendment.

It is regrettable that subsequent generations who picked up on Dr. Nott's theories knew nothing about their invalidity. Consequently, if a falsehood is repeated long enough, it becomes accepted as a truth. In 1883 a Missouri court heard the case of *State v. Jackson* and rendered a judgment based on mulatto sterility:

> It is stated as a well authenticated fact that if the issue of a black man and a white woman, and a white man and a black woman, intermarry, they cannot possibly have any progeny, and such a fact sufficiently justifies those laws which forbid the intermarriage of blacks and whites.

Over a hundred years after their inception, and long after slavery was abolished and proslavery propaganda was no longer needed, Dr. Nott's theories were still influential. In the 1948 California Supreme Court case *Perez v. Sharp* (also known as *Perez v. Lippold),* one of the dissenting judges stated:

> There is authority for the conclusion that the crossing of the primary races leads gradually to retrogression and to eventual destruction of the resultant type unless it is fortified by reunion with the parent stock.

This archaic thinking was limited to only one judge.

Inasmuch as we know with certainty that there are no adverse biological consequences inherent in the children of interracial marriages, it goes without saying that biracial children are just as intelligent, fecund, vital, and mortal as everyone else. All of the old literature was written for propaganda purposes only and had absolutely no basis in truth. Pushing the point of adverse biological consequences to the absurd, even the fall of the Roman Empire has been cited by some as being the result of interracial sexual relations; however, if Rome truly fell because of racial degeneracy, there would have been no Byzantine Empire. (Moreover, suggesting that the Roman Empire fell because of racial amalgamation is just as absurd as making the fall a women's issue, which has also been done!)

In contemporary American society, the subject of interracial marriage is frequently met with the question, "What about the children?" The fact is that interracial marriage is on the rise and more interracial children are being born. *What about the children?* Many professionals in the mental health field have found that psychological problems for interracial children are not inevitable. Alvin F. Poussaint, a professor of psychiatry at Harvard University, has conducted research on this issue and states, "It seems clear that a lot of the myths that a lot of people have about these children, their chances of success, their ability to cope, the capabilities of their parents, are just that — myths. All in all, they represent a rather successful group in this society." Thomas J. Buttery, an early childhood and elementary education specialist at the University of Alabama, agrees with fellow researcher Kate Shackford's assessment that teachers and social workers "frequently perceive children's problems as a result of the interracial nature of their families, when in fact they may be due to normal developmental stages or other problems that are unrelated to biracialness."

Perhaps this whole issue of racial amalgamation can best be summed up by the paleoanthropologists who have studied prehistoric mankind and agree that intermixing freely took place whenever migrations occurred. There are even the Grimaldi skeletons found in France from the Aurignacian period of 25,000 years ago that are said to have Negroid characteristics. If there was anything inherently detrimental in this prehistoric intermixing, human beings would have died out a long time ago and none of us would be here today. Moreover, even now in modern times, blood transfusions freely take place between all peoples. Many white Americans have the blood of Afro-Americans flowing in their veins and are not even aware of it. The same holds true from the genetic perspective. In 1958 sociologist Robert P. Stuckert conducted a genetic probability study and concluded, "Over twenty-eight million white persons are descendants of persons of African origin." In 1964 he revised the number to thirty-six million.

Chapter 9.   ARE WE LIVING OUT A LEGACY
                   FROM THE PAST?

   Thomas Anburey, *Travels Through the Interior Parts of America*
(1789; reprint, N. Y., 1969), 2:385; Edward S. Abdy, *Journal of a*
Residence and Tour in the United States of North America, from
April, 1833, to October, 1834 (1835; reprint, N. Y., 1969), 1:352-53;
Frederick Law Olmsted, *The Cotton Kingdom: A Traveller's Ob-*
servations on Cotton and Slavery in the American Slave States
(1861; reprint, ed. Arthur M. Schlesinger, N. Y., 1953), 235-36, 37,
229. Also, see Herbert Asbury, *The French Quarter* (N. Y., 1936),
125-35; "A Journey Through the South in 1836: Diary of James D.
Davidson," ed. Herbert A. Kellar, *Journal of Southern History* 1
(August 1935): 358; Harriet Martineau, *Society in America* (N. Y.,
1837), 2:116-17; James Parton, *General Butler in New Orleans*
(N. Y., 1864), 490; Frances Trollope, *Domestic Manners of the*
Americans (1832; reprint, ed. Donald Smalley, N. Y., Vintage
Books, 1949), 13-14; George Vandenhoff, *Leaves from an Actor's*
Note-Book (N. Y., 1860), 208.
   The concubinage system was not limited to free mulatto women.
Reverend Philo Tower who traveled three years through the Southern states wrote about beautiful slave women who were rented out
by their masters.   Although concubinage usually involved light-
complexioned mulattoes, such was not always the case.   Tower
wrote of respectable men in New Orleans "who take for their bed
companions not only the quadroons, – those who are only one-
fourth black blood, – but those of a darker hue, and frequently those
of the blackest shade, and live with them as with a wife, and by
whom they have large families." *Slavery Unmasked: Being a Truthful*
Narrative of a Three Years' Residence and Journeying in Eleven
Southern States (1856; reprint, N. Y., 1969), 316-27, quote on 322.
Besides its literal meaning, the term "quadroon (or quatroon)" had a
figurative meaning as well.   Isaac Holmes, an Englishman who
traveled in America, noted, "Although the term quatroon would
infer a person of three-fourths white extraction, yet all between the
colour of a mulatto and a white acquire in New Orleans this
appellation.   Some, indeed, are to all appearance perfectly white.
An Account of the United States of America (London, 1823), 333.
This same meaning can be found in J. Benwell, *An Englishman*

Travels in America: His Observations of Life and Manners in the Free and Slave States (London, [1853]), 205.

Anthropological Treatises of Johann Friedrich Blumenbach, ed. and trans. Thomas Bendyshe (London, 1865), 308-12, quote on 308; Johann David Schoepf, *Travels in the Confederation [1783-1784],* ed. and trans. Alfred J. Morrison (Phila., 1911), 2:152n; "James D. Davidson," 359; Helen Tunnicliff Catterall, ed., *Judicial Cases Concerning American Slavery and the Negro* (1926; reprint, N. Y., 1968), 2:530. For other contemporary references to the intelligence of blacks, see Abdy, *Residence and Tour* 2:216-17; *Annual Report of the American Anti-Slavery Society, by the Executive Committee, for the Year Ending May 1, 1859* (1860; reprint, N. Y., 1972), 76-78; Wilson Armistead, *A Tribute for the Negro* (1848; reprint, Westport, 1970); J[acques] P[ierre] Brissot de Warville, *New Travels in the United States of America, 1788,* trans. Mara S. Vamos, ed. Durand Echeverria (Cambridge, Mass., 1964), 217, 234-37. Other writers correctly pointed out that it was totally inappropriate to compare the *enslaved* mentality of the Negro with the *free* mentality of the white. Winthrop D. Jordan, *White Over Black: American Attitudes Toward the Negro, 1550-1812* (Chapel Hill, 1968), 283, 442-43.

Benjamin Rush, M.D., *Sixteen Introductory Lectures* (1811; reprint, Oceanside, N. Y., 1977), 117; Robert Brent Toplin, "Between Black and White: Attitudes Toward Southern Mulattoes, 1830-1861," *Journal of Southern History* 45 (May 1979): 185-96.

J. C. Nott, "The Mulatto a Hybrid - probable extermination of the two races if the Whites and Blacks are allowed to intermarry," *American Journal of the Medical Sciences,* n.s., 6 (July 1843): 252-56. A reprint appeared shortly after in the *Boston Medical and Surgical Journal* 29 (August 16, 1843): 29-32. For a challenge to Nott's theories, see G. Dorrance, "The Mulatto a Hybrid," *Boston Medical and Surgical Journal* 29 (August 30, 1843): 81. Coincidently, that same year George Tucker, a renowned Southern statistician and political economist, made reference to *mulatto longevity,* a concept totally contrary to those of Nott. *Progress of the United States in Population and Wealth in Fifty Years* (1855; reprint, N. Y., 1964), 69-70, 73. (Tucker published the first part of this book as a separate edition in 1843.) For the article which originally influenced Nott, see Philanthropist (pseud.), "Vital Statistics of Negroes and Mulattoes," *Boston Medical and Surgical*

Journal 27 (October 12, 1842): 168-70. Just one week after its publication, a supportive editorial called upon "mulatto inferiority" as the rationale for not repealing the Massachusetts law against interracial marriage (see Chapter 4). *Boston Medical and Surgical Journal* 27 (October 19, 1842): 192-93. Also, see William Stanton, *The Leopard's Spots: Scientific Attitudes Toward Race in America, 1815-59* (Chicago, Phoenix Books, 1960), 66-67. In addition to Toplin's article and Stanton's book, other references to Dr. Nott and his influence include George M. Fredrickson, *The Black Image in the White Mind: The Debate on Afro-American Character and Destiny, 1817-1914* (N. Y., 1971), chap. 3 and 161, 321; Thomas F. Gossett, *Race: The History of an Idea in America* (Dallas, 1963), 58-67; Reginald Horsman, *Josiah Nott of Mobile: Southerner, Physician, and Racial Theorist* (Baton Rouge, 1987); John G. Mencke, *Mulattoes and Race Mixture: American Attitudes and Images, 1865-1918* (Ann Arbor, 1979), 43-44, 50-52, 101-2.

Regarding the Bible and unified humanity, see for example, Acts 17.26 and Rom. 12.5. Although proslavery forces pointed to Biblical instances of slavery, they conveniently neglected Deut. 23.15-16. For related material, see Ron Bartour, "American Views on 'Biblical Slavery': 1835-1865, a Comparative Study," *Slavery and Abolition* 4 (May 1983): 41-55; Hinton Rowan Helper, *The Impending Crisis of the South: How to Meet It* (1857; reprint, ed. George M. Fredrickson, Cambridge, Mass., 1968), chap. 7; [Theodore D. Weld], *The Bible Against Slavery* (1864; reprint, Detroit 1970) and earlier editions in the 1830s. Mitchell Snay discusses the sanctification of slavery in "American Thought and Southern Distinctiveness: The Southern Clergy and the Sanctification of Slavery," *Civil War History* 35 (December 1989): 311-28.

Horsman, *Josiah Nott of Mobile,* 249; Samuel A. Cartwright "Diseases and Peculiarities of the Negro Race," *DeBow's Southern and Western Review* 11 (September 1851): 331-33.

For the version of Nott's theory, see J. D. B. DeBow, *The Commercial Review* 8 (June 1850): 588. An interesting comment regarding DeBow's appointment as census superintendent may be had in Frederick Law Olmsted, *Slavery and the South, 1852-1857* ed. Charles E. Beveridge and Charles Capen McLaughlin (Baltimore, 1981), 283.

In addition to the "passing" of nearly white free mulattoes a whites, illegal slave importations, and the wrongful enslavement of free blacks and free mulattoes, there was one minor influence on the census statistics which contributed to the "Free Colored" population decreasing, and that was emigration out of America. Some free blacks and free mulattoes went to Canada, Liberia (Africa), and Haiti, but their numbers were never really substantial. Regarding this emigration, see for example, Stanley W. Campbell, *The Slave Catchers: Enforcement of the Fugitive Slave Law, 1850-1860* (Chapel Hill, 1970), 62-63; "The Census," *United States Magazine, and Democratic Review* 25 (October 1849): 293; Tucker, *Progress of the United States,* 52, 68, 88, 93, 97.

J. D. B. DeBow, *Statistical View of the United States...A Compendium of the Seventh Census* (Washington, 1854), 62, and 64 for his comment on errors in the collection of census data for the "Free Colored" in Louisiana. For examples of runaway slaves with light complexions "passing" as white, see *Anti-Slavery Tracts. No. 2. White Slavery in the United States,* in *Anti-Slavery Tracts, Series 1: Nos. 1-20, 1855-1856* (Westport, 1970); L. Maria Child, *The Patriarchal Institution, as Described by Members of Its Own Family* (N. Y., 1860), 25-27; William Jay, *Miscellaneous Writings on Slavery* (1853; reprint, N. Y., 1968), 261-64; J. A. Rogers, *Sex and Race* (N. Y., 1942), 2:chaps. 19, 20. (Despite his texts being somewhat overzealous at times and occasionally inaccurate, the Rogers volumes are still excellent references for a wide range of primary sources.)

For the verbatim provisions of the 1807, 1819 and 1820 legislation, see Peter M. Bergman and Jean McCarroll, comps., *The Negro in the Congressional Record* (N. Y., 1970), 3:269-71, 6:319-20, 7:570-71. President Madison's statement and the difficulties of law enforcement may be had in Bergman and McCarroll, *Congressional Record* 7:215-18; W. E. Burghardt Du Bois, *The Suppression of the African Slave-Trade to the United States of America, 1638-1870* (1896; reprint, Baton Rouge, Louisiana Paperbacks, 1969), chap. 8; Donald L. Robinson, *Slavery in the Structure of American Politics, 1765-1820* (N. Y., 1971), 333-46.

Slave prices have been analyzed by Ulrich B. Phillips in his *American Negro Slavery* (1918; reprint, Baton Rouge, Louisiana Paperbacks, 1966), 370-75, particularly chart facing 370. The estimates for slave smuggling between 1815 and 1820 are cited in

Du Bois, *Suppression,* 124, and Robinson, *Slavery,* 338.

Regarding progeny and the internal slave trade, see James O. Breeden, ed., *Advice Among Masters: The Ideal in Slave Management in the Old South* (Westport, 1980), 286; Catterall, *Judicial Cases* 2:136, 392, 407, 579, and 3:138, 195; Henry Chase and C. H. Sanborn, *The North and the South: Being a Statistical View of the Condition of the Free and Slave States* (1857; reprint, Westport, 1970), 19-22; *Thomas Jefferson's Farm Book,* Edwin Morris Betts, ed. (Princeton, 1953), 43, 46; Harriet Beecher Stowe, *Uncle Tom's Cabin; or Life Among the Lowly* (1852; reprint, ed. John A. Woods, N. Y., 1965), 249; [Theodore D. Weld], *American Slavery as It Is: Testimony of a Thousand Witnesses* (1839; reprint, N. Y., 1968), 182-84; Olmsted, *Cotton Kingdom,* 45-48, 458n and his *Slavery and the South,* 250, 258; George M. Weston, *The Progress of Slavery in the United States* (1857; reprint, N. Y., 1969), 147-48. Also, Martineau, *Society in America* 2:112, 118. For other examples of Martineau's reference, see Anburey, *Travels* 2:386; *Narrative of the Life of Frederick Douglass an American Slave,* ed. Benjamin Quarles (1845; reprint, Cambridge, Mass., 1960), 26-27; [Janet Schaw], *Journal of a Lady of Quality,* ed. Evangeline W. Andrews (New Haven, 1923), 154; Robert Sutcliff, *Travels in Some Parts of North America in the Years 1804, 1805, & 1806* (London, 1811), 53, 95; [Theodore D. Weld], *Slavery and the Internal Slave Trade in the United States* (1841; reprint, N. Y., 1969), 32. Two good summaries of primary sources are to be found in the footnotes of Frederic Bancroft, *Slave-Trading in the Old South* (1931; reprint, N. Y., 1959), chap. 4, and Lewis Cecil Gray, *History of Agriculture in the Southern United States to 1860* (1932; reprint, Gloucester, Mass., 1958), 2:661-62 (despite the flawed text on 662-63).

In reference to the legal reopening of the African slave trade, it may be said that Southerners who already owned slaves had strong motivation for opposing such a move. Slaves offered a means by which capital would not only be preserved, but could appreciate as well, and a massive influx of new slaves would alter the supply side of the supply-demand equation causing a severe decline in slave prices.

For examples of slave smugglers who went unpunished, see Warren S. Howard, *American Slavers and the Federal Law, 1837-1862* (Westport, 1976), 224-35, and John R. Spears, *The American*

Slave-Trade: An Account of Its Origin, Growth and Suppression
(N. Y., 1900), 229-32. The comments of Douglas may be had in
*Annual Report of the American Anti-Slavery Society, by the
Executive Committee, for the Year Ending May 1, 1860* (1861;
reprint, N. Y., 1972), 20. Lincoln's party platform plank is listed in
Donald Bruce Johnson, comp., *National Party Platforms, 1840-
1956* (Urbana, 1978), 1:32-33. The Democratic party and the
Breckenridge faction of the Democratic party both included a
plank about the acquisition of Cuba in their 1860 political platforms. Can motives here be suspect inasmuch as Cuba is only
about one hundred miles off the coast of Florida, and Cuba at the
time was *the* slave smuggler's haven? (Of course, the Democratic
party of today is not only a unified party but is nothing at all like its
pre-Civil War ancestors. Likewise, the Republican party is quite
different as well.) The fact that the Republican party and the
Constitutional Union party did not include Cuba in their political platforms indicates that its acquisition was of sectional rather
than national importance. Johnson, *National Party Platforms*
1:30-33. Also, see *Annual Report of the American Anti-Slavery
Society, by the Executive Committee, for the Year Ending May 1,
1859* (1860; reprint, N. Y., 1972), 19-29. Du Bois, *Suppression,* 191
for the hanging reference.

Joseph C. G. Kennedy, *Population of the United States in 1860;
Compiled from the Original Returns of the Eighth Census* (Washington, 1864), viii-ix. J. D. B. DeBow who preceded Kennedy as
census superintendent acknowledged the existence of an illicit slave
trade but did not mention the United States in his comments.
Statistical View, 84. For his remarks on Florida and Louisiana, see
94.

The 1860 census commentary included Reichenbach's explanation about the natural increase in the slave population being
responsible for statistical anomalies. This view cannot be taken
seriously in light of the continuous number of illegal importations
to which President Madison first made reference in 1810. Kennedy,
Population, viii. Dr. Nott's comments regarding natural increase
must be considered in light of [Weld], *American Slavery,* banner
headline on 139 and census references on 140 and 142. J. C. Nott,
"Nature and Destiny of the Negro," *DeBow's Southern and Western Review* 10 (March 1851): 330. Slave mortality has been dis-

cussed in depth by Richard H. Steckel, "A Dreadful Childhood: The Excess Mortality of American Slaves," *Social Science History* 10 (Winter 1986): 427-65.

Estimates for post-1807 illegal slave importations are cited in Winfield H. Collins, *The Domestic Slave Trade of the Southern States* (1904; reprint, Port Washington, N. Y., 1969), 20, and W. E. B. Du Bois, "The Enforcement of the Slave-Trade Laws," in *Annual Report of the American Historical Association for the Year 1891* (Washington, 1892), 173. This total of about a quarter of a million may even be somewhat conservative in light of the figures for North and South American importations which Du Bois cited in his later work. *Suppression,* 142-43 and n. 1, also 179. In addition, see William Goodell, *Slavery and Anti-Slavery; A History of the Great Struggle in Both Hemispheres* (1852; reprint, N. Y., 1968), 67, and [Weld], *American Slavery,* 139-40. In 1846 Ezra C. Seaman, a well-known statistician and political economist, calculated that about 100,000 slaves were illegally imported into the United States between 1830 and 1840. *Essays on the Progress of Nations* (Detroit, 1846), 216, 403. Seaman's work has been examined in William L. Miller, "A Note on the Importance of the Interstate Slave Trade of the Ante Bellum South," *Journal of Political Economy* 73 (April 1965): 184.

Critics who claim that the quarter of a million figure for illegal slave importations is too high, point to the fact that many slaves who were exported from Africa landed in Cuba, not the Southern states. True enough, but the issue which goes unaddressed is where these slaves ultimately ended up. Many went to Brazil and South America, some remained in Cuba, etc., but what about the rest? When averaged out over the prohibition period from 1808 to 1860, the illegal importation of 250,000 slaves into the Southern states would only be about one hundred slaves per week. With the South clamoring for labor, domestic slaves in limited supply, slave prices high, poor enforcement of prohibitive legislation, and Cuba not far from the vast Southern coastline of the United States, is it realistic to think that slave smuggling did not occur to a considerable extent between Cuba and the Southern states? Historian Kenneth F. Kiple has stated that there was little to be gained financially in transferring slaves from Cuba to Florida because "slave prices in Cuba, Florida, and the southern United States as a whole closely approximated each other, from the termination of the United States slave trade right up to the beginning of the Civil War." The research of Ulrich B. Phillips, however, has established that different slave prices with disparities often in the hundreds of dollars existed in four Southern markets during this period. There *was* money to be made by slave traders buying slaves in Cuba and selling them in the South because, more often than not, slave prices in Cuba were lower than those in one or more of the Southern markets. Moreover, slave traders involved in larger operations could go to Africa, *buy direct,* and then use Cuba as a rest stop before smuggling their cargoes into the South. "The Case Against a Nineteenth-Century Cuba-Florida Slave Trade," *Florida Historical Quarterly* 49 (April 1971): 355; Phillips, *Negro Slavery,* 370 and tipped in chart. Hubert H. S. Aimes has compiled a list of Cuban slave prices, limited for the most part to newly imported slaves from Africa. *A History of Slavery in Cuba* (1907; reprint, N. Y., 1967), 267-68, also 170-71 and 245-48.

Warren S. Howard's calculations of the relatively small size of the African slave trade from 1857 to 1860 can not accurately account for the indeterminate number of *unknown* slave ships, particularly ordinary ships that were later converted for such use (not counting smaller craft which shuttled between Cuba and the U. S. coast). Howard also claims that very little slave smuggling occurred during the late 1850s by citing as evidence the fact that the 1870 census shows very few African-born blacks. This anomaly can readily be reconciled, however, by considering the consequences of congressional representation based on population. In the antebellum South, five slaves were counted as three freemen; in the postbellum South with slavery abolished, black men and white men were counted equally, provided they were American-born citizens and not foreign-born aliens. Inasmuch as ex-slaves who were born in Africa and smuggled into the United States could not be counted in a state's population of citizens on which congressional representation for that state was based, the Southern states had motivation to show as few African-born blacks as possible in the 1870 census. Of course, this was a relatively easy task given the widespread corruption which existed at that time throughout Reconstruction state governments. For Howard's views, see *American Slavers,* 255, 303. The instructions given to the assistant marshals who conducted the 1870 census underscore the importance of place of birth and congressional representation. Carroll D. Wright, *The History and Growth of the United States Census* (Washington, 1900), 158. Regarding the system of political patronage under which the 1870 census was conducted, see "The Census Imbroglio," *The Nation* 10 (February 24, 1870): 116-17.

There is an additional perspective to be viewed concerning illicit slave importations. Inasmuch as South Carolina seceded from the Union about a month after Lincoln was elected president in 1860, few would argue that the United States was a political powder keg in the late 1850s. In 1859, against this backdrop, President Buchanan's proslavery administration sent special agent Benjamin F. Slocumb to the South to report on whether or not there was any illegal slave importing activity going on. (Slocumb was sent by Jacob Thompson, secretary of the interior, who later resigned from the administration, organized Confederate army troops in Mississippi, and became a secret agent for Jefferson Davis.) Keeping in mind the political climate of the time, is it really any wonder that Slocumb reported that he found no evidence of slave smuggling? Moreover, this finding enabled President Buchanan to report to the nation on December 3, 1860, that "since the date of my last annual message not a single slave has been imported into the United States in violation of the laws prohibiting the African slave trade." The absolute character of this statement in itself seems sufficient to cast doubt on its validity. For Buchanan's remarks and Slocumb's report, see Robert Ralph Davis, Jr., "Buchanian Espionage: A Report on Illegal Slave Trading in the South in 1859," *Journal of Southern History* 37 (May 1971): 271-78, and Johnson, *National Party Platforms* 1:32, plank 5 for the proslavery bias of the Buchanan administration. A little over a week before Buchanan's report to the nation, the following appeared in a Virginia newspaper: "Cargoes of slaves have been landed at various times in the South, and the community tolerates their purchase and their presence on the cotton plantations." Dwight Lowell Dumond, ed., *Southern Editorials on Secession* (1931; reprint, Gloucester, Mass., 1964), 262. Also, see J. E. Cairnes, *The Slave Power: Its Character, Career, and Probable Designs* (1862; reprint, N. Y., 1969), 124, and R. R. Madden, *The Island of Cuba* (London, 1853), 90. A Florida newspaper brazenly admitted, "We of the slave States care but little, if anything, for suppressing the slave trade." *Floridian and Journal,* 23 June 1860, p. 2.

More on illicit slave importations may be had in *Annual Reports of the American Anti-Slavery Society, by the Executive Committee, for the Years Ending May 1, 1857, and May 1, 1858* (1859; reprint, N. Y., 1972), 53-58 and 120-23, *...for the Year Ending May 1, 1859,* 37-61, *...for the Year Ending May 1, 1860,* 13-30, *...for the Year Ending May 1, 1861,* 126-40; Barton J. Bernstein, "Southern Politics and Attempts to Reopen the African Slave Trade," *Journal of Negro History* 51 (January 1966): 29; W. O. Blake, *The History of Slavery and the Slave Trade, Ancient and Modern* (1858; reprint, N. Y., 1969), 2:chaps. 17-19; George M. Brooke, Jr., "The Role of the United States Navy in the Suppression of the African Slave Trade," *American Neptune* 21 (January 1961): 28-41; Thomas Fowell Buxton, *The African Slave Trade and Its Remedy* (1840; reprint, London, 1967), 40-59; *Captain Canot; or, Twenty Years of an African Slaver,* ed. Brantz Mayer (1854; reprint, N. Y., 1968) and the comments of Mabel M. Smythe in Théophile Conneau, *A Slaver's Log Book, or 20 Years' Residence in Africa* (Englewood Cliffs, N. J., 1976), iii-xi; [George Washington Carleton], *The Suppressed Book about Slavery! Prepared for Publication in 1857, - Never Published Until the Present Time* (1864; reprint, N. Y., 1968), 408-12; *Revelations of a Slave Smuggler: Being the Autobiography of Capt. Rich'd Drake, an African Trader for Fifty Years - From 1807 to 1857* (1860; reprint, Northbrook, Ill., 1972); Goodell, *Slavery and Anti-Slavery,* 251-62; Jay, *Miscellaneous Writings,* 274-303; Daniel P. Mannix and Malcolm Cowley, *Black Cargoes: A History of the Atlantic Slave Trade, 1518-1865* (N. Y., Compass Books, 1965), chaps. 9-12; Robert Royal Russel, *Economic Aspects of Southern Sectionalism 1840-1861* (1924; reprint, N. Y., 1960), 215; Hugh G. Soulsby, *The Right of Search and the Slave Trade in Anglo-American Relations, 1814-1862* (Baltimore, 1933); *Southern Cultivator* 17 (March 1859): 70; Spears, *American Slave-Trade;* David Turnbull, *Travels in the West. Cuba; with Notices of Porto Rico, and the Slave Trade* (1840; reprint, N. Y., 1969); [Weld], *Slavery,* 248-51; Tom Henderson Wells, *The Slave Ship "Wanderer"* (Athens, 1967), 52; Laura A. White, "The South in the 1850's as Seen by British Consuls," *Journal of Southern History* 1 (February 1935): 36-41; Harvey Wish, "The Revival of the African

Slave Trade in the United States, 1856-1860," *Mississippi Valley Historical Review* 27 (March 1941): 582-86.

[Weld], *American Slavery,* 140-42, quote on 142 (italics in original). The Fugitive Slave Act of 1850 never really accomplished very much. Stanley W. Campbell, perhaps the leading authority on this subject, stated, "Many Southerners felt that, as long as a majority in the North remained hostile to the institution of slavery and the recovery of fugitive slaves, the law was unenforceable....During the period 1850 through 1860, 191 slaves were claimed in the federal courts under the Fugitive Slave Law....At considerable trouble and expense, a minority of the cases, or 43.3 percent, required the return of the slaves by federal marshals." The point to keep in mind is that appearance before a federal court to reclaim a fugitive slave was really just a formality because *any* black or mulatto, free or slave, could readily be claimed and abducted with no legal recourse. Furthermore, the Act provided severe penalties for anyone obstructing the pursuit of a fugitive slave (or one said to be a fugitive slave). These included $1,000 fine, six months imprisonment, and another $1,000 if the fugitive was not recaptured due to the intervention. In terms of 1850's dollars, $1,000 was a very large sum of money considering that the daily wages paid to a day laborer in the aggregate of all states and territories averaged $1.11 at that time. Campbell, *The Slave Catchers: Enforcement of the Fugitive Slave Law, 1850-1860* (Chapel Hill, 1970), quotes on 148 and 167. Samuel May, Jr., *The Fugitive Slave Law and Its Victims* (1861; reprint, Freeport, N. Y., 1970), quote on 3 and 3-4 for synopsis of the law. May only cited from kidnapping cases *which had become public.* His work can be put into perspective with this analogy: these days we hear about illicit drug shipments that are intercepted by the authorities, but the question is, how many such shipments are not intercepted and never heard about? Wilbur H Siebert, *The Underground Railroad from Slavery to Freedom* (N. Y., 1898), 361-66 for the law in full. Regarding wages, see DeBow, *Statistical View,* 164.

G. W. Featherstonhaugh, *Excursion Through the Slave States* (London, 1844), 2:267 (italics added); [Carleton], *Suppressed Book,* 24, 42-43, 94, 280-81, 295-97, 300-1, 314, 327-28, 330-33, 335, 340-41, 348-49, and 93-94, 288-89, 293.

More on kidnapping may be had in E. A. Andrews, *Slavery and the Domestic Slave-Trade in the United States* (1836; reprint, Detroit, [1969]), 150, 184-85; *Annual Report...for the Year Ending May 1, 1859,* 69-76, *...for the Year Ending May 1, 1860,* 36-43, *...for the Year Ending May 1, 1861,* 142-52; Campbell, *Slave Catchers,* 44-45, 175; [Carleton], *Suppressed Book,* 288, 329, 416; William Chambers, *American Slavery and Colour* (1857; reprint, N. Y., 1968), 186-88, 192-94; Collins, *Domestic Slave Trade,* chap. 5; Goodell, *Slavery and Anti-Slavery,* 141-42, also 318, 413 and n.; [Weld], *American Slavery,* 140-42; and for example, Benwell, *Englishman's Travels,* 207. For an overview of legislation passed in an attempt to counter kidnapping, see Norman L. Rosenberg, "Personal Liberty Laws and Sectional Crisis: 1850-1861," *Civil War History* 17 (March 1971): 25-44. Details are discussed in Thomas D. Morris, *Free Men All: The Personal Liberty Laws of the North, 1780-1861* (Baltimore, 1974).

Paul H. Buck, "The Poor Whites of the Ante-bellum South," *American Historical Review* 31 (October 1925): 41-54; A. N. J. Den Hollander, "The Tradition of 'Poor Whites'," in *Culture in the South,* ed. W. T. Couch (Chapel Hill, 1935). Dodd worded his estimate as follows: "A thousand families received over $50,000,000 a year, while all the remaining 666,000 families received only about $60,000,000." William E. Dodd, *The Cotton Kingdom: A Chronicle of the Old South* (N. Y., 1919), 24. Wages computed from *Statistics of the United States, (Including Mortality, Property, &c.,) in 1860; Compiled from the Original Returns and Being the Final Exhibit of the Eighth Census* (Washington, 1866), 512. Also, see Edgar W. Martin, *The Standard of Living in 1860: American Consumption Levels on the Eve of the Civil War* (Chicago, 1942), 393, 407-16. Slave prices are in Phillips, *Negro Slavery,* 370 and tipped in chart. Overall profit potentials become apparent when slave prices throughout the antebellum period are compared and contrasted with the wages paid to farm hands, common labor, and skilled labor during that time. Stanley Lebergott, "Wage Trends, 1800-1900," in Conference on Research in Income and Wealth, *Trends in the American Economy in the Nineteenth Century,* vol. 24 of *Studies in Income and Wealth* (Princeton, 1960), 462.

African slave costs, expenses, and profits are cited in Buxton, *African Slave Trade,* 221-25; *Captain Canot,* 87, 100-1; [Carleton], *Suppressed Book,* 413-14; Howard, *American Slavers,* 2, 236-37,

265; Madden, *Island of Cuba,* 34; *Revelations of a Slave Smuggler,* 99-100; Turnbull, *Travels,* 368-69, 424. For Cuba and the Louisiana, Virginia, and Texas references, see Alexander Jones, *Cuba in 1851* (N. Y., 1851), 20, 23; Basil Rauch, *American Interest in Cuba: 1848-1855* (1948; reprint, N. Y., 1974), 203 along with observations on 200 and 206; Turnbull, *Travels,* 64 and 149 for quotes, also 171, 391. Wages are in DeBow, *Statistical View,* 164, and Lebergott, "Wage Trends," 462.

Jay, *Miscellaneous Writings,* 389-93, quote on 389, also see 236-47; Harriet Beecher Stowe, *The Key to Uncle Tom's Cabin; Presenting the Original Facts and Documents Upon Which the Story Is Founded* (1854; reprint, N. Y., 1968), 340-45, quote on 340. The influence that the illegal slave trade had on census figures was recognized back in the 1830s. [Weld], *American Slavery,* 140, 142.

The 1840 and 1850 census figures show the "Free Colored" population going down while at the same time slave prices in general were going up. It is true that slave prices fell between 1837 and 1844, however, this dip straddled these two censuses and thus spread the price impact over two decades. Kennedy, *Population,* ix; Phillips, *Negro Slavery,* chart facing 370.

The three-fifths compromise is in the third clause of ARTICLE I, SECTION 2 of the U. S. Constitution. For historical development, see *The Records of the Federal Convention of 1787,* ed. Max Farrand with index by David M. Matteson (New Haven, 1966), 4:108. Nathaniel Weyl and William Marina, *American Statesmen on Slavery and the Negro* (New Rochelle, 1971), 50-51; Chase and Sanborn, *The North and the South,* 24-28, quote on 26n. Also, see Cairnes, *Slave Power,* 100-1; [Carleton], *Suppressed Book,* 3-4, 22-23; Chambers, *American Slavery,* 88, 167-68; Goodell, *Slavery and Anti-Slavery,* 134-35; Robinson, *Slavery,* 405-6, 427.

It can be argued that slavery gained in political power as it lost in agricultural importance. Using 1850 census data, contemporary statisticians Henry Chase and C. H. Sanborn figured, *"The North, with half as much land under cultivation, and two-thirds as many persons engaged in farming, produces two hundred and twenty-seven millions of dollars worth of agricultural products in a year more than the South; twice as much on an acre, and more than double the value per head for every person engaged in farming."* *The North and the South,* 41 (italics in original).

More on the "Slave Power" may be had in David Brion Davis, *The Slave Power Conspiracy and the Paranoid Style* (Baton Rouge, 1970); Russel B. Nye, "The Slave Power Conspiracy: 1830-1860," *Science and Society* 10 (Summer 1946): 262-74; Mark W. Summers, *The Plundering Generation: Corruption and the Crisis of the Union, 1849-1861* (N. Y., 1987), 215-35, 241, 251, 257, 276. Of course, there really was no "Slave Power" conspiracy per se. Political needs and wants of the South in general, slavery in particular, bonded Southern congressmen together out of common necessity. The "Slave Power" was an alliance rather than a literal conspiracy.

The *influence* of the "Slave Power," however, is not to be underestimated. The extent of this influence can be seen in the interpretation of President Buchanan's severe illness at the National Hotel in Washington as an attempted assassination by poisoning. Although a disease of some sort appeared at the National Hotel in January of 1857, prior to Buchanan's arrival, some believed that such illness could have been used to cover up an intentional poisoning by the "Slave Power." John Smith Dye, *History of the Plots and Crimes of the Great Conspiracy to Overthrow Liberty in America* (N. Y., 1866), 90-94; Davis, *Slave Power Conspiracy,* 7-10 and 88 n. 5 for contemporary references, along with the additional entries in *The New York Times Index for the Published News of September 1851 - December 1862* (N. Y., 1967), 164; David C. Mearns, *The Lincoln Papers* (Garden City, N. Y., 1948), 1:283-87. Another example of the influence the "Slave Power" had can be seen in Lincoln's famous "A House Divided" speech in which he alludes to the phenomenon. *The Collected Works of Abraham Lincoln,* ed. Roy P. Basler (New Brunswick, N. J., 1953), 2:461-69. The context of Lincoln's position has been developed in Harry V. Jaffa, *Crisis of the House Divided: An Interpretation of the Issues in the Lincoln-Douglas Debates* (N. Y., 1959), chaps. 11 and 12. Also worth noting here was the attempt to impose slavery on the free territory of Kansas. See Orville J. Victor, *History of American Conspiracies* (1863; reprint, N. Y., 1969), 451-520.

J. D. B. DeBow, *The Commercial Review* 8 (February 1850): 203 for quote and 8 (March 1850): 293n for an interesting comment about census takers. Regarding the slavery issue and errors in the 1840 census, see DeBow, *Statistical View,* 76 and 113 (Table 115); Edward Jarvis, J. Wingate Thornton, Wm. Brigham, "The Sixth

Census of the United States," *Hunt's Merchants' Magazine* 12 (February 1845): 133-37; House Select Committee on Statistics, *Last Census -- Errors,* 28th Cong., 1st sess., 17 June 1844, H. Rept. 579 and *Errors in Sixth Census,* H. Rept. 580; Frederick Merk, *Slavery and the Annexation of Texas* (N. Y., 1972), 61-68, 85-92, 112-13, 117-20; Stanton, *Leopard's Spots,* 58-65; Tucker, *Progress of the United States,* 25A.

The *Works of John C. Calhoun,* ed. Richard K. Crallé (N. Y., 1855), 5:337-39, 458-61. *Memoirs of John Quincy Adams, Comprising Portions of His Diary from 1795 to 1848,* ed. Charles Francis Adams (1874-77; reprint, N. Y., 1970), 12:29 for quote, and also 22-23, 36. One page later he offers this lament: "The deepest of my afflictions is the degeneracy of my country from the principles which gave her existence, and the ruin irreparable of them all, under the transcendent power of slavery and the slave-representation." Stowe, *Key to Uncle Tom's Cabin,* 505-8, quote on 507-8 (all italics in original); Albert Deutsch, "The First U. S. Census of the Insane (1840) and Its Use as Pro-Slavery Propaganda," *Bulletin of the History of Medicine* 15 (May 1944): 469-82, quote on 478. In 1839 statistician Archibald Russell suggested that by addressing the issue of slavery in more detail in the upcoming census of 1840, "we would learn the amount and extent of the domestic slave trade in this country." Not unexpectedly, his recommendation went unheeded. Russell, *Principles of Statistical Inquiry; as Illustrated in Proposals for...the Census to Be Taken in 1840* (N. Y., 1839), 143-45, quote on 144.

Tucker, *Progress of the United States,* 28A. In order to really understand the extent to which illiteracy existed in the South prior to the Civil War, it is worthwhile citing some data. According to the native white population and literacy figures in the census of 1850 only one out of every four hundred New Englanders over twenty years of age was unable to read and write. The number was one in forty for the nonslaveholding states and one in twelve for the slave states. Contemporary statisticians Henry Chase and C. H. Sanborn pointed out that in some slave states illiteracy was particularly high, citing one in seven for South Carolina, one in five for Virginia, and one in three for North Carolina. They state, "Indeed, if we compare the *entire* number attending all Schools (Colleges, Academies private and public Schools), we find...more than four-fifths of the

children attending School in the Union are in the free States."
DeBow, *Statistical View,* 153; Chase and Sanborn, *The North and
the South,* 96 (italics in original), 103-4. For more on pre-Civil War
Southern illiteracy, see DeBow, *The Commercial Review* 8
(February 1850): 205; [Carleton], *Suppressed Book,* 24-25, 238, 248;
Clement Eaton, *The Freedom-of-Thought Struggle in the Old
South* (N. Y., Harper Torchbooks, 1964), chap. 3; Hinton Rowan
Helper, a Southern author, attributed the illiteracy of the South to
slavery in his *Impending Crisis,* 376-82, 404-8; Frederick Law
Olmsted, *A Journey in the Seaboard Slave States* (N. Y., 1856),
245-46n; Tucker, *Progress of the United States,* 146.

   Regarding illiteracy and public opinion, in 1854 Frederick Law
Olmsted wrote, "It is true that but a small proportion of the people
of the South have this personal interest in wresting power from the
North, but this small proportion have the *money power,* and the
ignorance and stupidity of the poorer class at the South is so great
that it possesses the means of almost absolute control of public
opinion." *Slavery and the South,* 285 (italics in original). For his
travels, *Cotton Kingdom,* 229, 459-60. John S. Wilson's quote may
be had in Breeden, *Advice Among Masters,* 220 (italics in original).
Also, see Catterall, *Judicial Cases* 1:231.

   L[ouisa] S. M[cCord], "Uncle Tom's Cabin," *Southern Quarterly Review* 23 (January 1853): 90 (italics in original), 117-18,
and Thomas F. Gossett, *UNCLE TOM'S CABIN and American
Culture* (Dallas, 1985), 109, 112, 190, 205-6. In 1856 Dr. Nott and
several other prominent men of Mobile, Alabama society ran two
booksellers out of town for being involved with *Uncle Tom's Cabin* and other "objectionable" works. Horsman, *Josiah Nott of
Mobile,* 223-24; *Annual Reports...for the Years Ending May 1,
1857, and May 1, 1858,* 6-9; [Carleton], *Suppressed Book,* 248-50.
For the newspaper references, see Howard Cecil Perkins, ed.,
Northern Editorials on Secession (1942; reprint, Gloucester, Mass.,
1964), 1:472, 476, and also the example in Harold M. Hyman,
"Election of 1864," in *History of American Presidential Elections,
1789-1968,* ed. Arthur M. Schlesinger, Jr. et al. (N. Y., 1971),
2:1230.

   Joel Williamson, *New People: Miscegenation and Mulattoes in
the United States* (N. Y., 1984), 65-67. For a celebrated case of
interracial marriage, see William G. Allen, *The American Prejudice*

Against Color. An Authentic Narrative, Showing How Easily the Nation Got into an Uproar (1853; reprint, N. Y., 1969), and also Chambers, *American Slavery,* 188-90. Regarding Dr. Nott's inability to prove his theories, see Horsman, *Josiah Nott of Mobile,* 87, 96, 99, 196, 205-6, 217, 300; Thomas L. Nichols, *Forty Years of American Life* (1864; reprint, N. Y., 1969), 2:236-38. Nott's influence was also felt in France. Joy Harvey, "Nineteenth-Century French Responses to Southern U. S. Physicians' Views on Race and Hybridity" (Paper presented at 54th Annual Meeting of the Southern Historical Association, Norfolk, Virginia, 10 November 1988).

Kennedy, *Population,* xi (all italics added). The two censuses of which Kennedy speaks are 1850 and 1860. Regarding the inclusion of mulattoes in the former, see J. D. B. DeBow, *The Commercial Review* 8 (June 1850): 587-88. Also, see Bureau of the Census, *Negro Population in the United States, 1790-1915* (Washington, 1918), 207. I am indebted to Margaret C. O'Brien of the American Sociological Association who first called my attention to the fact that historical censuses are valuable as social documents. Although our conclusions differ, her point is well-taken. Parker G. Marden, Jeffry R. Gibson, and Margaret C. O'Brien, "The Census as a Social Document: Changes in the Concept of 'Race': 1790-1870" (Paper to be read at "Sociology and History" Section of the Annual Meeting of the American Sociological Association, San Francisco, California, 28-31 August 1967).

There is an intriguing discrepancy in the 1860 census publications of 1862 and 1864. In the *Preliminary Report on the Eighth Census, 1860* published in 1862, Kennedy concluded, "In a simple statement, when viewed apart from the liberations or manumission in the Southern states, the aggregate free colored in this country must represent *nearly* what is termed 'a stationary population,' characterized by an equality of the current of births and deaths." (According to Dr. Nott, the mulatto population could never have equality of births and deaths and would eventually die out because of frailty and sterility.) In the *Population of the United States in 1860* published in 1864, Kennedy altered his previous point of view by stating, "These developments of the census, to a good degree, explain the slow progress of the free colored population in the Northern states, and indicate, with unerring certainty, the *gradual extinction* of that people the more rapidly as, *whether free or slave,* they become diffused among the dominant race." Kennedy made his 1862 statement before all the data were tabulated, however, this is all the more significant in light of the fact that the 1862 figure for "Free Colored" increase was 10.97% compared to a higher 12.32% in 1864. *For Kennedy's statements to accord with his statistics, these two figures should have been reversed. Preliminary Report,* 6 (italics in original); *Population,* xi (italics added).

Congressional Globe, 39th Cong., 1st sess., 2 April 1866, 1721-23, quote on 1722; House Committee on Printing, *Joseph C. G. Kennedy,* 39th Cong., 1st sess., 23 April 1866, H. Rept. 50; *Daily Constitutional Union,* 21 Oct. 1865, p. 1; House Committee of Claims, *Joseph C. G. Kennedy,* 38th Cong., 1st sess., 4 March 1864, H. Rept. 28, 2. An earlier report also found no problem with Kennedy's salary. Senate Committee on Claims, *Joseph C. G. Kennedy,* 36th Cong., 1st sess., 10 April 1860, S. Rept. 182. Further evidence that Kennedy was stopped right in the midst of his work may be found on the errata page of *Manufactures of the United States in 1860; Compiled from the Original Returns of the Eighth Census* (Washington, 1865). *Statistics of the United States...the Eighth Census,* 287 for the Jarvis quote.

For the case concerning Kennedy's alleged disloyalty, see House Committee on the Judiciary, *J. C. G. Kennedy,* 37th Cong., 3d sess., 29 Jan. 1863, H. Rept. 19.

When Dr. Nott compared 1840 census statistics and found that the rate of increase for the "Free Colored" population (comprised of numerous mulattoes) was less than that for other population groups, he explained the difference in terms of his "mulatto inferiority" theories. Although modern scholars have analyzed these same census statistics and others and have offered different explanations, no one has addressed the issue in terms of statistical distortions being primarily based on nearly white mulattoes "passing" over into white society as whites, illegal slave importations, and kidnapping.

A good example is that of the eminent historian Lewis Cecil Gray who paints a dismal picture of free blacks and free mulattoes "in the greater portion of the ante bellum South" and concludes, "Their general wretchedness was probably reflected in statistics of net rate of increase, which in four out of seven decades was less than the rate for Negro population as a whole [all blacks and mulattoes, free and slave], in spite of the additions through manumission." This is a generalization. Gray does not explain why the other three decades show increases. *History of Agriculture* 1:524, and also 2:650, 938. Moreover, wretchedness existed in the Negro population among both free *and* slave, and in terms of statistics, the deaths of wretched free blacks and free mulattoes were not influenced by any external factor except for a small amount of manumissions, whereas the deaths of wretched slaves were tempered by illicit accretions.

The kidnapping of juveniles is another aspect of the "Free Colored" population decline that has not received the attention it deserves. First, keep in mind that in 1860 the wages paid to a day laborer averaged $1.18 *and* that the Fugitive Slave Act of 1850 virtually condoned kidnapping by suspending the civil rights of free blacks and free mulattoes. Next, add the fact that in the slave markets from 1850 to 1860, prices for *children under ten years of age* were in the hundreds of dollars (not to mention that even back in 1835 a boy of about seven or eight was worth up to $400). The combination of these elements appears to suggest that the abduction of free blacks and free mulattoes under ten years of age contributed to the lower census numbers for the "Free Colored" aggregate. Historian Ira Berlin does not consider this factor in his statistical computations. *Slaves Without Masters: The Free Negro in the Antebellum South* (N. Y., 1974), 175 n. 61. Among the many references which address the value of children, see Bancroft, *Slave-Trading,* 78, 79 n. 33, 116, 208-13, 350-52, 357-58 nn. 47, 48; [Carleton], *Suppressed Book,* 152, 157, 162, 258; Gray, *History of Agriculture* 2:664; Phillips, *Negro Slavery,* 370; Parton, *General Butler,* 490; Andrews, *Slavery and the Domestic Slave-Trade,* 147. For wages, see *Statistics of the United States...the Eighth Census,* 512.

Among the antislavery pressures of the 1850s were the following: 1850 - the Fugitive Slave Act which put free blacks and free mulattoes in jeopardy of being wrongfully enslaved; 1852 - the widespread publication of *Uncle Tom's Cabin* by Harriet Beecher Stowe, a novel which depicted nearly white mulattoes and the horrors of slavery; 1854 - the passage of the Kansas-Nebraska Act which opened up the possibility of slavery expansion into the territories; 1857 - the Dred Scott decision in which the U. S.

Supreme Court ruled that a slave did not become a citizen even though he had lived on free soil; 1859 - the Southern Commercial Convention at Vicksburg, Miss. which wanted the repeal of all laws prohibiting foreign slave trade. That such antislavery pressures were intense early in the decade is exemplified by South Carolina's belligerent posture. See Ashley Halsey, Jr., "South Carolina Began Preparing for War in 1851," *Civil War Times Illustrated* 1 (April 1962): 8-13. A microcosm of the tension which existed between the North and the South during the 1850s can be seen in the attack by South Carolina Congressman Preston S. Brooks on Massachusetts Senator Charles Sumner in 1856. Sumner had given a speech in which he chastised Brooks's uncle, South Carolina Senator Andrew P. Butler. Two days later, as a matter of Southern honor, Brooks went to the Senate chamber after adjournment and repeatedly clubbed Sumner over the head with a gutta percha cane. Brooks wrote that Sumner received "about 30 first rate stripes" and that "I wore my cane out completely but saved the Head which is gold." The trauma Sumner experienced kept him from returning to the Senate for over three years. *Much more significant than the attack itself was the South's reaction to it.* Instead of being the object of outrage, Brooks was lauded. He noted, "The fragments of the stick are begged for as *sacred relicts* [relics]." Southern congressmen supported his action, and the two-thirds vote necessary to expel him from Congress was not obtained. Brooks resigned but was immediately re-elected, receiving widespread public support throughout much of the South along with resolutions of approval and gifts of new gold-headed canes. David Donald, *Charles Sumner and the Coming of the Civil War* (N. Y., 1960), chaps. 11 and 12, quotes on 295 and 304 (italics in original); Chambers, *American Slavery,* 99-114; *Dictionary of American Biography,* s.v. "Brooks, Preston Smith."

Regarding abolition and amalgamation, see for example, Eugene H. Berwanger, *The Frontier Against Slavery: Western Anti-Negro Prejudice and the Slavery Extension Controversy* (Urbana, Illini Books Edition, 1971), 36, 128-34; [Carleton], *Suppressed Book,* 251; Colonel John Eaton, Jr., *Report of the General Superintendent of Freedmen, Department of the Tennessee and State of Arkansas, for 1864* (Memphis, 1865), 94; Elliott, *Sinfulness of American Slavery* 1:152-53; Tucker, *Progress of the United States,*

117. The view in the North that equated abolition with amalgamation was developed long before the 1850s. Leonard L. Richards, *"Gentlemen of Property and Standing": Anti-Abolition Mobs in Jacksonian America* (N. Y., Galaxy Books, 1971), 30-32, 40-45, 71, 114-15, 120-23, 155, 166.

As the election of 1860 approached, the promulgation of Dr. Nott's "mulatto inferiority" theories really heated up. Talk reached a feverous pitch concerning whites and mulattoes intermarrying, producing inferior offspring, and thereby jeopardizing the whole white population. Perhaps the one publication which best exemplified this unbridled paranoia was the desperate article "Amalgamation" by W. W. Wright of New Orleans which appeared just ten months prior to the start of the Civil War. *DeBow's Review* 29 (July 1860): 1-20.

Collected Works 2:405 (italics in original); David Ruggles, *The "Extinguisher" Extinguished! or David M. Reese, M. D. "Used Up."* (N. Y., 1834), 12, 14; James Kinney, *Amalgamation! Race, Sex, and Rhetoric in the Nineteenth-Century American Novel* (Westport, 1985), 235-37. Other relevant literature includes *Incidents in the Life of a Slave Girl* (1861) by Harriet A. Jacobs, a short story by Louisa May Alcott entitled "M. L." (1863), a work often omitted from her standard anthologies, and Lydia M. Child's *A Romance of the Republic* (1867). This interracial genre has continued into the twentieth century. See Christopher D. Geist, "Violence, Passion, and Sexual Racism: The Plantation Novel in the 1970s," *Southern Quarterly* 18 (Winter 1980): 60-72.

"Miscegenation" (from the Latin *miscere,* mix, and *genus,* race) was first introduced into the English language by journalist Croly and Wakeman. Their pamphlet was so widely read that their neologism "miscegenation" replaced "amalgamation" as the popular denotation for interracial sex or marriage. The term is still used as the formal word for interracial sexual relations. The *Miscegenation* hoax had such a profound impact that P. T. Barnum even included it in his book, *The Humbugs of the World* (1865; reprint, Detroit, 1970), chap. 33. For more on the background and consequences of the pamphlet, see J. M. Bloch, *Miscegenation, Melaleukation, and Mr. Lincoln's Dog* (N. Y., 1958); Sidney Kaplan, "The Miscegenation Issue in the Election of 1864," *Journal of Negro History* 3 (July 1949): 274-343; Forrest G. Wood, *Black Scare: The Racist*

Response to Emancipation and Reconstruction (Berkeley, 1970), chap. 4. In addition to the *Miscegenation* pamphlet, "The Lincoln Catechism" was another anti-Lincoln publication which attempted to influence the presidential election of 1864 by playing upon the interracial issue. Hyman, "Election of 1864," 1230.

Alfred Avins, "Anti-Miscegenation Laws and the Fourteenth Amendment: The Original Intent," *Virginia Law Review* 52 (October 1966): 1224-55, and R. Carter Pittman, "The Fourteenth Amendment: Its Intended Effect on Anti-Miscegenation Laws," *North Carolina Law Review* 43 (1964): 92-109.

For court cases, see Lloyd H. Riley, "Miscegenation Statutes - A Re-evaluation of Their Constitutionality in Light of Changing Social and Political Conditions," *Southern California Law Review* 32 (Fall 1958): 37; Robert J. Sickels, *Race, Marriage, and the Law* (Albuquerque, 1972), 99.

Any modern objective text dealing with race attests to biological equality. For example, UNESCO, *Race, Science and Society,* ed. Leo Kuper, (N. Y., 1975). Notable earlier accounts include E. W. Gifford, "Race Mixture," *University of California Chronicle* 31 (1929): 72-78, and Franz Boas, "Race and Progress," *Science* 74 (July 3, 1931): 1-8. Also, see Thomas F. Pettigrew, *A Profile of the Negro American* (Princeton, 1964), 62-64.

Regarding the fall of the Roman Empire as a women's issue, see Vern L. Bullough, *The Subordinate Sex: A History of Attitudes Toward Women* (Baltimore, Penguin Books, 1974), chap. 4. For general arguments, see Norman H. Baynes, "The Decline of the Roman Power in Western Europe. Some Modern Explanations," *Journal of Roman Studies* 33 (1943): 29-35; Shepard B. Clough, *The Rise and Fall of Civilization: An Inquiry into the Relationship between Economic Development and Civilization* (N. Y., 1957), chap. 5; S. N. Eisenstadt, ed., *The Decline of Empires* (Englewood Cliffs, N. J., 1967). A comprehensive annotated bibliography may be had in Alden M. Rollins, comp., *The Fall of Rome: A REFERENCE GUIDE* (Jefferson, N. C., 1983).

Alvin F. Poussaint, "Study of Interracial Children Presents Positive Picture," *Interracial Books for Children Bulletin* 15 (no. 6, 1984): 10. This issue also contains similar views by Joyce Ladner, "Providing a Healthy Environment for Interracial Children"; Kate Shackford, "Interracial Children: Growing Up Healthy in an

Unhealthy Society"; and Philip Spivey, "Communicating Is the Key." Thomas J. Buttery, "Biracial Children: Racial Identification, Self-Esteem and School Adjustment," *Kappa Delta Pi Record* 23 (Winter 1987): 50-53, quote on 50 (condensed in *Education Digest* 52 [May 1987]: 38-41).

Regarding the Grimaldi skeletons, see Alan Houghton Brodrick, *Man and His Ancestry* (London, 1960), 211, 232-33; Legrand Clegg II, "The First Invaders," in *African Presence in Early Europe,* ed. Ivan Van Sertima (New Brunswick, N. J., 1985), 23-35; Arthur Keith, *Ancient Types of Man* (N. Y., 1911), chap. 6; Henry Fairfield Osborn, *Men of the Old Stone Age: Their Environment, Life and Art,* 3d ed. (N. Y., 1921), 262-69; Eugène Pittard, *Race and History,* trans. V. C. C. Collum (N. Y., 1926), 67-72; J. A. Rogers, *Sex and Race* (N. Y., 1942), 1:31-36 and his *Nature Knows No Color-Line,* 3d ed. (N. Y., 1952), 15-16.

Robert P. Stuckert, "African Ancestry of the White American Population," *Ohio Journal of Science* 58 (May 1958): 160 and "Race Mixture: The African Ancestry of White Americans," in *Physical Anthropology and Archaeology, Selected Readings,* ed. Peter B. Hammond (N. Y., 1964), 196.

10

WHERE DO WE GO FROM HERE?

Nearly one-half (47%) of the white women in the national probability sample agreed that in the field of sexuality, interracial sexuality is a very worthwhile subject for future research (Belief Statement 10). The data obtained show that white women are willing to share their beliefs regarding interracial sexuality, that various beliefs do indeed exist, and that there is much interest in the issues which were addressed. Although the public opinion survey presented in Part One focused exclusively on the current beliefs of white women, the beliefs of white men, black women, and black men are just as valid and merit professional attention as well. Surveys addressing these groups (as well as repeated samplings of white women) offer many opportunities for future research.

Various demographic groups within the national sample of white women showed particularly interesting preliminary findings. The blue collar workers and the not married group had divergent agreement rates regarding interracial sexual fantasy, as did the South regarding interracial dating. The incomplete high school education or less group showed many atypical responses. Those 18-24 and those 65 and over generally differed in response rates throughout the survey, suggesting that a woman's age has an influence on her beliefs about interracial sexuality.

Some demographic groups were small, so the issue to be addressed in this regard is whether repeated samplings would support or refute the initial data that were obtained. Moreover, conducting repeated samplings of all the demographic groups over time would monitor the development of any trends in the beliefs of individual groups as well as the collective national sample. Inasmuch as this present study is the first of its kind, how will its various findings be viewed historically?

As revealed in the survey data, 41% of the white women believed that many white men view their own sexuality as being somehow different than that of Afro-American men. Upon what is such a belief based? What behaviors have white men exhibited that white women have perceived? Perhaps these questions suggest the issue of penis anxiety, however, it just may be that in many cases some *other* sexual anxiety is being perceived. A survey conducted by Ellen Berscheid, et al. in *Psychology Today* found that "to our considerable surprise, only 15 percent of the men worry about the size of their penises; barely six percent are very dissatisfied." To what extent is the low level of penis anxiety expressed by the readership of this periodical typical or atypical? Is penis anxiety an idea that has been accurately portrayed in the professional literature?

Other possibilities for future research are suggested by the findings for the belief about interracial sexual fantasy. Although the professional literature is lacking in any writings which exclusively address this issue, new material could be developed by taking what is known about the psychosexual dynamics and motivations of sexual fantasy in general and then applying that knowledge to interracial sexual fantasy in particular. Many psychoanalytic inquiries would surely address the Oedipus complex to a greater or lesser extent.

If the Oedipus complex is to retain its credence in contemporary American society where divorce is becoming commonplace, articles need to be written in the professional literature which reconcile the two-parent Oedipal ideal with the one-parent Oedipal reality. Such articles would be particularly significant regarding girls because most one-parent households are headed by women, and the same-sex Oedipal dynamic between a mother and a daughter is an intricate one. What role do older and/or younger siblings play in the Oedipal development of a girl in a mother or father single-parent household? How about Oedipal development in stepfamilies where there are two father figures? Do different possible family constellations modify traditional Oedipal development and influence a girl's choice of partners for dating and marriage? The classic Oedipus complex was based on the nuclear family of child-mother-father, however, at present the nuclear family is rapidly changing. Can new psychoanalytic patterns be discerned for the formulation of a neo-Oedipus paradigm? If so, would any new criteria underlie a white woman having interracial sexual relations?

Another survey finding suggests further inquiry. Although 43% of the national sample agreed with the belief about interracial sexual relations being at the root of racial prejudice in America today, 40% disagreed. Racial prejudice in and of itself was out of the scope of this book, however, social and behavioral scientists might well want to ask white women what they believe *is* at the root of the racial prejudice which exists in America. If not ultimately interracial sexual relations, then what?

The subject of interracial sexuality has been viewed from psychological perspectives, but are there philosophical perspectives which are applicable as well? Beliefs, attitudes, values, and mores are all inextricably bound together. How does each influence the whole of which it is a part? Is a pragmatic perspective possible? What other points of view might also be considered?

In terms of future research, many of the current historical perspectives on interracial sexual relations and related issues are in need of a second look. Much forgotten American history, a legitimate part of the past nonetheless, has been discussed in this book. Why has so much of this history not been made available to the general public until now? What is the responsibility of the historian in terms of presenting an accurate account or at least presenting both sides of controversial historical subject matter? The illicit importation of slaves from Cuba and Africa is an excellent example. Slave smuggling was outlawed as of January 1, 1808. If such activity virtually ceased, why did Congress pass additional legislation in 1819 *and* 1820? Furthermore, if there was no slave smuggling to speak of, why did Lincoln's party make "the African slave trade" a political issue in 1860? Instead of *acknowledging the possibility* that sizable illegal slave importations could have taken place, many historians who have studied American history state that such activity was either minimal or virtually nonexistent. Considering the profits involved and the clandestine nature of smuggling, how can they speak with such certainty? The census of 1840 is another example of sensitive American history that has been mistreated. The article by Albert Deutsch accurately described the facts of how falsified census figures were accepted and used as proslavery propaganda. Why was such an article found in the *medical* literature and not in the American history literature? The antislavery movement is yet another historical issue that has been dealt with inaccurately. Why do many historians insist on explaining away the legitimate arguments of abolitionists as being nothing more than the propaganda of irrational zealots? Historian W. E. B. Du Bois has referred to history as "lies agreed upon." However unintentional, have historians been blinded by a psychology of imitation?

Unfortunately, many historians have not applied the concept of "contextualism" to their work. Contextualism states that for a part to have meaning, it must be evaluated in terms of the whole of which it is a part, or as John Dewey scholar Richard J. Bernstein says, "The background of a context qualifies the material in the foreground." From a historical perspective, to consider interracial sexual relations out of the *social context* in which they occurred, is to consider a part out of its whole. This issue as well as others pertaining to the subject of interracial sexuality have been so hopelessly misrepresented that a contextual approach offers many opportunities for future revisionist work.

Sociology and psychology are the other academic disciplines in which research on interracial sexuality will be conducted in the future, research that will undoubtedly raise new questions and suggest new answers. Public opinion surveys and related endeavors will play a major role in providing data for sociologists and psychologists as their disciplines move toward a deeper understanding of the dynamics of interracial sexual relations and the degree to which society at large accepts these relationships. Throughout this book it has been seen how yesterday has influenced today. Looking ahead, one wonders how today will influence tomorrow....

Chapter 10. WHERE DO WE GO FROM HERE?

Ellen Berscheid, Elaine Walster, and George Bohrnstedt, "Body Image. The Happy American Body: A Survey Report," *Psychology Today* 7 (November 1973): 121.

In a paper published in 1931, psychoanalyst Otto Fenichel began to address the Oedipus complex in configurations other than the traditional triangle of child-mother-father. His ideas, however, remain to be fully developed. "Specific Forms of the Oedipus Complex," in *The Collected Papers of Otto Fenichel: First Series* (N. Y., 1953), chap. 22. Robert R. Sears, *Survey of Objective Studies of Psychoanalytic Concepts* (1943; reprint, Millwood, N. Y., 1978), 136-37.

A number of contemporary nonfiction books (of greater or lesser literary value) suggest that interracial sexual relations has been and continues to be at the root of racial prejudice. See Beth Day, *Sexual Life Between Blacks and Whites: The Roots of Racism* (N. Y., 1972); Grace Halsell, *Black/White Sex* (N. Y., 1972); Fernando Henriques, *Children of Conflict: A Study of Interracial Sex and Marriage* (N. Y., 1975); Calvin C. Hernton, *Sex and Racism in America* (N. Y., 1965); J. A. Rogers, *Sex and Race*, 3 vols. (N. Y., 1940-1944); Charles Herbert Stember, *Sexual Racism: The Emotional Barrier to an Integrated Society* (N. Y., 1976); Doris Y. Wilkinson, ed., *Black Male/White Female: Perspectives on Interracial Marriage and Courtship* (Cambridge, Mass., 1975).

Donald Bruce Johnson, comp., *National Party Platforms, 1840-1956* (Urbana, 1978), 1:32; Albert Deutsch, "The First U. S. Census of the Insane (1840) and Its Use as Pro-Slavery Propaganda," *Bulletin of the History of Medicine* 15 (May 1944): 469-82; W. E. B. Du Bois, *Black Reconstruction in America* (1935; reprint, N. Y., 1969), 714.

John Dewey, *On Experience, Nature, and Freedom: Representative Selections,* ed. Richard J. Bernstein (N. Y., Library of Liberal Arts, 1960), 88. Also, see Stephen C. Pepper, *World Hypotheses: A Study in Evidence* (Berkeley, 1970), chap. 10.

APPENDIX

Much has been said in Chapter 9 regarding the United States census of 1860 and its official statistics and commentary for the "Free Colored" population. It is important to note, however, that the biased treatment which this particular group received was not an isolated case. There are two other groups in the 1860 census (as well as in the 1850 census for that matter) that warrant a second look: the manumitted (freed) slaves and the fugitive (runaway) slaves. In addition to the "Free Colored," the official statistics and commentaries for these other groups are also worthy of attention because they provide two more examples of how (as Harriet Beecher Stowe had stated previously) the United States census was again being used as a proslavery propaganda document.

During periods when the "Free Colored" population increase was small, slave prices were high and manumissions were not popular. Historian Whittington B. Johnson has observed that the South's "reliance on slave labor, which, with its consequent increase in slave prices, tended to discourage manumissions." By 1860 Louisiana, Georgia, Mississippi, and Alabama had outlawed them altogether. Joseph C. G. Kennedy, superintendent of the 1860 census, spoke of "the 20,000 manumissions which are believed to have occurred in the past ten years." From 1850 to 1860, manumission was legally difficult if not impossible, and slave prices were soaring to unbelievable new heights. Where did the 20,000 manumissions for this decade come from? Furthermore, according to Kennedy, "By the Eighth Census, it appears that manumissions have greatly increased in number in Alabama, Georgia, Louisiana, Maryland, Mississippi, North Carolina, and Tennessee." Why would manumissions have "greatly increased in number" in four states where such action was *outright illegal* by 1860?

Census figures for fugitive slaves present yet another anomaly. The slave populations in the censuses of 1850 and 1860 were recorded at 3,204,313 and 3,950,531 respectively, yet the figures for fugitive slaves were only 1,011 for 1850 and 803 for 1860, *about one-thirtieth of one percent and one-fiftieth of one percent.* Superintendent Kennedy states, "It will scarcely be alleged that these returns are no reliable, being, as they are, made by the persons directly interested, who would be no more likely to err in the number lost than in those retained." Are the small census figures for fugitive slaves truly accurate?

An important part of proslavery propaganda from about 1830 onward was that slaves had no desire for freedom because they were happy and content with their lot in life. Historian Larry E. Tise has surveyed antebellum proslavery literature and has identified several interconnected major propaganda themes which were designed to show the slave in a state of contentment. These themes were "slavery not irksome to men who never knew freedom" (referring to slavery from birth), "Negro happier enslaved than free," "labor protected against every contingency of life," and "provide comforts of life." The whole idea was to show those who opposed slavery that slaves were contented. To admit to large numbers of runaway slaves was to admit that the slaves were *not* contented, and such admissions were to be avoided at all costs because they could be used by the North as an antislavery argument. Large numbers of fugitive slaves did force the South to go public with the problem, but rather than admit that their "contented" slaves had run away from slavery on their own, other explanations were sought. As referred to earlier, Dr. Samuel A. Cartwright came up with Drapetomania, "the disease causing Negroes to run away." Occasionally, a Southern politician would blame Northern abolitionists for being responsible for the fugitive slave problem; however, had involving the abolitionists been a valid argument, it would have received much more support from Southern politicians in general. Even if abolitionists were involved as claimed, the slaves who were aided became fugitives and their numbers should have shown up in the census statistics for fugitive slaves.

The idea of the contented slave was an important part of Southern propaganda, and it is most significant that Southern politicians ever admitted in congressional discussions that the South had experienced great slave losses due to runaways. These losses must have been extreme, despite the small official census statistics to the contrary, and this state of affairs explains the reason Southern politicians breached their own propaganda line. *Those who would argue that fugitive slaves did not number in many thousands must reconcile this breaching with the small census figures for fugitive slaves*. The slave power may have breached its propaganda line, but in the end the line remained intact. Just as the 1840 census was used as a propaganda instrument by the South, the same may be said of the 1850 and 1860 censuses with their small "official government numbers" for the fugitive slaves. Proslavery forces were able to show these figures to the public at large in the North and claim with *official proof* that indeed fugitive slaves were few in number, the implication being that the slaves were happy and content with life and had no desire to be free. Breaching the propaganda line and small census figures could coexist in the context of those days due to the fact that census publications were widely circulated whereas the printed records of congressional discussions were not.

Superintendent Kennedy must have felt compelled to defend the small number of fugitive slaves given in the 1860 census because he stated, "Fortunately, however, other means exist of proving the correctness of the results ascertained." Comparing the population figures for the "Free Colored" in the free states with the population figures for the "Slaves," Kennedy reasoned that if many slaves were running away to the free states, the number of "Free Colored" in those states would have been much larger and the "Slave" population would have shown a decrease as the result of such losses. Kennedy seems to have overlooked one crucial issue of common sense, and that is, "What fugitive slave would want to talk to a strange white man (the census enumerator) asking a lot of questions?" No doubt many of these slaves went underground at the time of the census in order to further distance themselves from the *threat* if not the reality of abduction. The same may be said of those who fled to Canada and the Canadian censuses as well. Kennedy made one last point in defense of the fugitive slave figures in the 1860 census. He stated that "the slaves have increased 23½ per cent., presenting a natural augmentation altogether conclusive against much loss by escapes; the natural increase being equal to that of the most favored nations, irrespective of immigration, and greater than that of any country in Europe for the same period." The large increase in the slave population had nothing whatsoever to do with a lack of fugitive slaves or an extraordinary number of progeny. The increase was due to accretions from illegally imported new slaves and the wrongful enslavement of free blacks and free mulattoes.

What may be said about the actual number of fugitive slaves?

Although exact figures cannot be determined, historian Wilbur H. Siebert has done research on this subject in his book *The Underground Railroad from Slavery to Freedom* (1898) and has concluded that the official census figures are entirely inaccurate. Siebert interviewed many surviving abolitionists who ostensibly worked for the underground railroad and supplemented these accounts with a great deal of convincing secondary material. Whatever may be said of Siebert's study, either through the help of the organized underground railroad per se or independent antislavery sympathizers, fugitive slaves did escape from the South into the free states of the North and Canada, thousands more than official census figures indicated. Historian Ronnie C. Tyler has pointed out that thousands also escaped into the safe haven of Mexico. Just to illustrate how ridiculous the official statistics were, the census of 1850 cited the number of fugitive slaves from Texas for that year at 29, and the number cited in the census of 1860 was even lower at 16.

One last point remains to be addressed regarding the census statistics for fugitive slaves. It was very difficult for a slave to escape from the deep South, yet slaveholders from that area still complained of runaways. Inasmuch as slaves were worth a great deal of money, the absence of many can readily be explained in terms of slave stealing. While it is true that some missing slaves were known to have been stolen, others who were stolen without their master's knowledge must have been thought to be runaways and their numbers should have shown up in the census statistics for fugitive slaves. However, once again, the statistics remained small.

Given the politics of slavery days, it should surprise no one that with proslavery forces in control of the Federal government, the census of 1860 was manipulated and utilized as a proslavery propaganda document. According to its misleading statistics and commentaries, the "Free Colored" population declined because of "mulatto inferiority," more slaves were being given their freedom through an increasing amount of manumissions, and there were very few slaves who became fugitives by absconding from their bondage.

For Stowe's reference to the official United States census being used as a proslavery propaganda document, see *The Key to Uncle Tom's Cabin; Presenting the Original Facts and Documents Upon Which the Story Is Founded* (1854; reprint, N. Y., 1968), 506-8.

Whittington B. Johnson, "Manumission," in *Dictionary of Afro-American Slavery,* ed. Randall M. Miller and John David Smith (N. Y., 1988), 431-32; Joseph C. G. Kennedy, *Population of the United States in 1860; Compiled from the Original Returns of the Eighth Census* (Washington, 1864), xv-xvi. Also, see George Tucker, *Progress of the United States in Population and Wealth in Fifty Years* (1855; reprint, N. Y., 1964), 52, 118, and especially 12A. A comparative manumission chart for 1850 and 1860 may be had in Joseph C. G. Kennedy, *Preliminary Report on the Eighth Census, 1860* (Washington, 1862), 137.

For census statistics and commentary regarding fugitive slaves, see Kennedy, *Population,* xvi and *Preliminary Report,* 137. Larry E. Tise, *Proslavery: A History of the Defense of Slavery in America, 1701-1840* (Athens, Ga., 1987), 109-10, 112, 121, 244 (unnumbered), and for instance, Kenneth S. Greenberg, *Masters and Statesmen: The Political Culture of American Slavery* (Baltimore, 1985), 98-99, or Lillian Adele Kibler, *Benjamin F. Perry: South Carolina Unionist* (Durham, 1946), 282. A good example of the abolitionist argument is located in *Congressional Globe,* 31st Cong., 1st sess., 6 March 1850, Appendix, 340.

Wilbur H. Siebert, *The Underground Railroad from Slavery to Freedom* (N. Y., 1898), 312-13, 340-42, 351 for public admissions of Southern politicians; xiii, 342-43 for comments on the census; 220-22, 237, 346 for Canada and other numbers; 11-13, 351 for respondents. Also, see *The Anti-Slavery Bugle,* 4 Oct. 1851, p. 1. Ronnie C. Tyler, "Fugitive Slaves in Mexico," *Journal of Negro History* 57 (January 1972): 1-12; Kennedy, *Preliminary Report,* 137.

Slave stealing had a long history. For eighteenth and early nineteenth-century references, see Ulrich B. Phillips, *American Negro Slavery* (1918; reprint, Baton Rouge, Louisiana Paperbacks, 1966), 381-82. Two particular techniques are described in James Lal Penick, Jr., "John A. Murrell: A Legend of the Old Southwest," *Tennessee Historical Quarterly* 48 (Fall 1989): 174, 180.

Concluding Remarks

The imagination is the mechanism of the mind which makes incomplete thinking complete. When a curiosity exists, the mind demands an answer to the question that is posed, and in the absence of knowledge, the mental process of imagination provides that answer, true or not. Aristotle and other ancients who sought to answer how white women married to white men could have mulatto babies, came up with the theories of "atavism" and "maternal impression." Dr. Nott who sought to justify nearly white mulattoes continuing to be enslaved, came up with his frailty and sterility theories of "mulatto inferiority." All of these theories were the false answers of the imagination but were believed in the absence of knowledge. The subject of interracial sexuality is just as vulnerable to the influence of the imagination as anything else is, perhaps even more so in light of the paucity of information available on the various issues to which it relates. The book you have just read has been an attempt to clarify misunderstandings by replacing imagination with knowledge.

In light of the extremely complex and multifaceted nature of interracial sexuality, the commentaries in Part Two dealt with particular subject matter, and other perspectives necessarily went unaddressed. That fact notwithstanding, *A Completely New Look at Interracial Sexuality* has been a contribution in pushing back the frontier of social science, particularly in the areas of public opinion research and sociohistorical interpretation.

As stated previously, the discussion of interracial sexual relations is not the promotion of same. An honest effort has been made to discuss factual information, and hopefully this has been accomplished. May this book and others like it contribute to a better understanding among *all* people and, in the words of President Bush, to "a kinder and gentler nation."

Photo Sources

1. Foto Marburg/Art Resource, New York
   Philippa Catanensis, fol. 347 of Cod. gall. 6
   Boccaccio, *Des cas des nobles hommes et femmes*
   Munich, Bayerische Staatsbibliothek

2. Giraudon/Art Resource, New York
   Bosch, *Garden of Earthly Delights,*
   Center panel: Allegory of Luxuria (PFC 4643)
   Madrid, Prado

3. Details from PLATE 2

4. Bildarchiv Preussischer Kulturbesitz
   Lucius Septimius Severus and family
   Berlin, Antikenmuseum
   Staatliche Museen Preussischer Kulturbesitz

5. Giraudon/Art Resource, New York
   Greek Janiform aryballos (LA 21872)
   Paris, Louvre

6. Leonard von Matt/Photo Researchers, New York
   Satyr mit Mädchen (FA 1252)
   Naples, Museo Archeologico Nazionale

7. M. Yacoub, *Guide du Musée de Sfax* (Tunis, 1966)
   Mosaïque funéraire païenne
   Plate 14, figs. 2, 3 (inverted)
   Sfax, Musée de Sfax

8. Rare Books and Manuscripts Division
   Massachusetts placard
   The New York Public Library
   Astor, Lenox and Tilden Foundations

9. State Historical Society of Wisconsin
   Wisconsin placard

10. Rare Books and Manuscripts Division
    Republican party handbill
    The New York Public Library
    Astor, Lenox and Tilden Foundations

11. United States Census of 1860
    Title pages from original census documents